Gestalt

The Gestalt Therapy Page is the Internet's oldest and most comprehensive web resource for information, resources, and publications relating to the theory and practice of Gestalt therapy.

Visitors can subscribe to News and Notes, a free email calendar of conferences, training programs, and other events of interest to the worldwide Gestalt therapy community.

The Gestalt Therapy Page includes an on-line store that offers the most comprehensive collection of books and recordings available – many available nowhere else!

Visit today: www.gestalt.org

The Gestalt Journal Press was founded in 1975 and is currently the leading publisher and distributor of books, journals, and educational recordings relating to the theory and practice of Gestalt therapy. Our list of titles includes new editions of all the classic works by Frederick Perls, Laura Perls, Paul Goodman, Ralph Hefferline, and Jan Christiaan Smuts. Our catalog also includes a wide variety of books by contemporary theoreticians and clinicians including Richard Hycner, Lynne Jacobs, Violet Oaklander, Peter Philippson, Erving & Miriam Polster, Edward W. L. Smith, and Gary Yontef.

In 1976, we began publication of The Gestalt Journal (now the International Gestalt Journal), the first professional periodical devoted exclusively to the theory and practice of Gestalt therapy.

Our collection of video and audio recordings features the works of Frederick (Fritz) and Laura Perls, Violet Oaklander, Erving & Miriam Polster, Janie Rhyne, and James Simkin.

The Gestalt Journal Press, in conjunction with the University of California, Santa Barbara, maintains the world's largest archive of Gestalt therapy related materials including original manuscripts and correspondence, published and unpublished, by Gestalt therapy pioneers Frederick & Laura Perls and Paul Goodman. The archives also include more than sixty thousand hours of audio and video recordings of presentations, panels and interviews dating to early 1961.

On the Occasion of an Other

JEAN-MARIE ROBINE

A Publication of The Gestalt Journal Press

Published by:

    The Gestalt Journal Press, Inc.

    P. O. Box 278

    Gouldsboro, ME 04607

ISBN # 978-0-939266-71-5

Contents

PART 2

Acknowledgments

Many others were *occasions* for the construction of these ideas and I want to thank them for our encounters and conversations.

In particular . . . .

from the United States: Isadore From, Sonia Nevis, Michael V. Miller, Gary Yontef, Erving and Miriam Polster, Philip Lichtenberg, Lynne Jacobs, Douglas Davidove, Gordon Wheeler, Ed and Barbara Lynch . . . .

and from France, Belgium and Québec: Marie Petit, André Jacques, Jean Gagnon, André Lamy, Jacques Blaize, Nicole de Schrevel, Brigitte Lapeyronnie, Jean and Jacqueline Broustra.

I am indebted to Karen Vincent-Jones, Gordon Wheeler, and Bettina Bergo who are responsible for the translations. Their skills aided in producing the most accurate edition possible.

A special thanks to my editor and publisher, Joe Wysong. His complete works, journals and books have been with me since the first issue of *The Gestalt Journal* in 1978 and were my primary source of Gestalt therapy theoretical nourishment.

Many others made significant contributions to this book without knowing it. Some were the writers and thinkers quoted throughout the book.

Most important were my students whose comments on my teaching and their challenging and unsettling questions were, and still are, my primary trainers.

— Jean-Marie Robine

FOREWORD
by Michael Vincent Miller

The brilliant innovations of Gestalt therapy — its relinquishing of the Freudian unconscious for a holistic, field-oriented conception of human nature and its redirecting the therapy session from an archeological hunt for causality to creative improvisations in the present moment of the session itself — first appeared more than fifty years ago. They have not on the whole been followed by equally brilliant further elaboration and development. Perhaps the followers of most intellectual or cultural movements rarely approximate the creativity of its founders. Nevertheless the population of Gestalt therapists continues to expand, even though the movement has carried on pretty much from the sidelines. Gestalt therapy training institutes exist in numerous countries on several continents. Some of them flourish, though most struggle to survive. There are a growing number of journals and conferences devoted to Gestalt therapy. Yet no more than a handful of teachers, thinkers, and writers among Gestalt therapists have succeeded in extending very far the lines of inquiry that were first opened when this beautiful groundbreaking theory and practice originally appeared. Among this small group Jean-Marie Robine, who lives in Bordeaux, France (though he teaches all over the world like a therapeutic nomad with an urgent mission) stands out as one of the most inventive and important figures on the current scene.

Robine's special gift as a theorist is a sensibility that moves with ease from the philosopher's absorption in the task of fine-tuning concepts to the clinician's fascination with the nuances of feeling and behavior. One doesn't find many such sensibilities in the annals of psychological theory. William James (although he wasn't a therapist, he had the eye and intuition of a good clinician), Freud himself, the phenomenological psychiatrists Ludwig Binswanger, Medard Boss, J. Van den Berg, and Erwin Straus, as well as the idiosyncratic Jacques Lacan come to mind. A weave of philosophical acumen with therapeutic finesse seems like an ideal combination of talents for the making of new psychological theory. In this regard one might recall that psychology was considered a branch of philosophy until well into the nineteenth century. But just as psychotherapy was being invented, it became captive to a new social development, the breaking up of professions into specialized secular priesthoods. Both psychotherapy and psychological theory fell under the sway of a medical outlook. Gestalt therapy, however, at least when it was first developed, remained on intimate terms with philosophy. The experience of reading the opening chapters of the volume that Goodman contributed to Perls, Hefferline, and Goodman, *Gestalt Ther apy: Excitement and Growth in the Human Personality* is more like coming across a new book by James or Bergson or Merleau-Ponty than it is like reading a conventional psychology textbook or a psychoanalytic monograph (later in the book, the tone and style change somewhat, as the influence of ego psychology gains a heavier grip).

Then a strange thing happened to Gestalt therapy on its way to California in the 1960s. Under the charismatic leadership of Frederick Perls, who left his more literary and philosophically inclined collaborators (including his wife Laura along with Paul Goodman and Isadore From) in New York, Gestalt therapy took on some of the character of an evangelical spiritual movement. In this form it had a moment of rather wide popularity. This version might well be called vulgar Gestalt therapy, because it resembles Perls's and Goodman's original vision about as much as what is called vulgar Marxism resembles the writings of Karl Marx. Live in the Here and Now, Take Responsibility for Your Feelings, I am I, and You are You, proclaimed this version of Gestalt therapy. Perfectly sound slogans, to be sure, but impatient, reductive ones, and they offer the practitioner little guidance for the painstakingly intricate and contemplative work of attending to another person's difficulties and untapped possibilities. This was a misfortune not only for Gestalt therapy but for the progress of psychotherapy in general. The message of Perls, Hefferline, and Goodman was lost for the most part in the American enthusiasm for quick fixes (even though Perls himself finally warned against them) and thus disregarded by the majority of clinicians outside Gestalt therapy's immediate circles. The misfortune continues to be transmitted widely in our own day.

Robine has always been deeply committed to Gestalt therapy, but the very nature of his commitment was bound to lead him in a different direction from 1960s Gestalt therapy. He is a radical thinker in the best sense of the word — the kind of radical who opens new frontiers by first going to the root (which is what the word radical actually means). We tend to think of radicals as being so far to the left in breaking with traditional politics or culture as to be off the map. In fact, the best radicals have a conservative streak. They are likely to see present establishments as bureaucratized corruptions of valuable traditions — for example, traditions of freedom or excellence. Going to the root involves a return to origins to recover a spirit or a set of values that has been lost. Robine makes his own radical departure through going back with a fine-tooth comb to the original text of Perls, Hefferline, and Goodman, as well as to the thinkers who influenced Perls and Goodman, such as Otto Rank, Kurt Lewin, and John Dewey. In this pursuit he rather reminds one of Jacques Lacan in his famous return to Freud. Lacan attempted to peel away layers of superficiality and mediocrity that had grown up around Freud's writings in order to investigate their very basis. Robine has done something similar with Goodman. The result is to produce radically new possibilities by bringing to the foreground implications that were overlooked or ignored by generations of followers.

The novelty of Robine's ideas stems partly from the fact that no such going back is merely a return to the past. In his theoretical writings, Robine continually tests the principles of Perls, Hefferline, and Goodman against both his own temperament and the changes that have taken place in western culture since that book first appeared. It is pertinent in this respect that Robine happens to be French. Philosophy as well as the arts took a major turn during the second half of the last century from modernism to what became known as postmodernism. In those branches of thought most relevant to psychology and psychotherapy, this turn moved the center of gravity from Germany and the United States, where the influence of Freud, Husserl, Heidegger, Buber, and Lewin and their American counterparts, such as James and Dewey (to name the ones most relevant to Gestalt therapy) dominated, to France, where Lacan, Merleau-Ponty, Levinas, Derrida, and Deleuze recomposed what they learned from their German ancestors into new paradigms. Robine has filtered Gestalt therapy through the thought of both these groups, going back to those who influenced Perls and Goodman, as well as forward to the more recent group of his countrymen (not including Lacan, in whom Robine exhibits no interest).

Why bring the complications of modern philosophy to bear on psychotherapy? Doesn't this just make the life of the psychotherapist more difficult? No doubt, but the vicissitudes of human existence are themselves subtle and difficult to understand. A common tendency in therapy is to reduce them to determinisms, such as claims that mental disturbance is all biology or childhood trauma or bad conditioning. Such therapy does not begin to address either the complication or the creativity of our psychic lives. This seems a particularly important point to make in our era. In inventing psychoanalysis, Freud drew on an ancient philosophical tradition of Socratic self-knowledge. His idea of relieving mental suffering entailed a discipline of exploring oneself in the presence of a skilled empathic listener and interpreter. This has long been a culturally dominant view of psychotherapy, but it is currently struggling against increasing medicalization and rationalization of health services which are affecting therapeutic practice everywhere. The Socratic may be in danger of fading away, at least in clinical and hospital settings. To preserve the Socratic tradition means bringing philosophy as much as psychological or neurological research to bear on psychotherapy. I think that Robine would agree with me that the best psychotherapy is a kind of applied philosophy.

As I have already suggested, Gestalt therapy lends itself particularly well to a philosophical emphasis. Gestalt therapy subjected what it took from psychoanalysis not only to Gestalt psychology but also to a phenomenological and existentialist outlook with a liberal dose of American pragmatism added to the mix. This gave rise to a mode of practice in which the psychotherapist closely observes, using the therapy session itself as a staging place, how patients confer their own special expressive styles (including symptoms) upon both their experience of themselves and their worlds or, more accurately, their experience of themselves *in* their worlds. Most Gestalt therapists adhere to this principle in practice. But much of Gestalt therapy theory has not kept up. The literature of Gestalt therapy after Perls, Hefferline, and Goodman, especially in English, is strewn with references to "the patients' phenomenology" or "our phenomenological approach," as though it can be taken for granted that everyone knows what these phrases mean. How can you coherently extend an idea into new territory when you take it for granted in a superficial way? If you invoke philosophy at the level of theory, you need to take seriously what the relevant philosophers say. Yet Robine, who has brought to bear on Gestalt therapy theory an encyclopedic knowledge of phenomenological and existential-phenomenological philosophy, has not had a lot of company in this endeavor.

Among other things Robine's borrowings from philosophy support a principle that to some is now an old-fashioned idea — that awareness is the prerequisite of therapeutic change. Self-knowledge is, of course, basic to the Socratic tradition, and it was basic to psychoanalysis' notion that knowing oneself is healing. This has traditionally been taken to imply an introspective search, a journey inward. But here Robine, carrying forward certain implications in Gestalt therapy, makes a fundamental change in point of view. The psychoanalytic enterprise originally concentrated on understanding the individual patient's inner life, with its unconscious conflicts, its blocked instinctual drives, and its mechanisms of defense. More recently psychoanalytic practice and theory has come ever closer to the Gestalt therapy theory of fifty years ago (without acknowledging its predecessor) by focusing on the relational and intersubjective aspects of human conduct. Robine, however, finds themes in Goodman's work that lead him to take Gestalt therapy well beyond, or more precisely, to a stage in the making of experience well before, the relational and intersubjective perspectives. Although relational and intersubjective psychoanalytic therapies shift attention in varying degrees from the patient's inner life to the relationship between patient and therapist, both assume that such relationship is between selves already individualized into something like finished products.

Robine, however, assumes no such thing. He has never cared much about finished products in psychology. Especially in his recent work both theory and practice begin without preconceptions about individualized selves or established roles. But if it is not the individual self — or even the relational or intersubjective self — that is the subject matter of psychology, what is? And how does this bear on the practice of psychotherapy? The basis for an answer to these questions is already to be found in Goodman's opening remarks in Perls, Hefferline, and Goodman. Goodman writes, "We speak of the organism contacting the environment, but it is the contact that is the simplest and first reality" (1994 [1951], p. 3). In other words, "contact," defined as the continuous, active, fluctuating meetings between organism and environment, is itself the proper and primary subject of psychology. The implication here is that psychological experience is located neither inside the person as a combination of drives and mental representations of an external world, nor in interactions between a sub-jective self and an objective world, but in active meetings be-tween the person and a world in which he or she is already embedded — that is, in meetings in which each is shaping the other and from which neither can be separated from the other without profound impoverishment of experience and loss of meaning.

Robine began to examine and elaborate these ideas in "Contact — the First Experience," one of the early essays (1990) not included in this collection. He made it clear that, for Gestalt therapy, contact — the very act of meeting — pre-cedes anything that might be understood as a relationship, whether defined in terms of object relations or from an existen-tial dialogical standpoint (intersubjectivity). If contacting, then, is the primary phenomenon in human mental life, it is to this activity itself that psychological theory and the practice of psychotherapy must direct its attention. In bringing this out, Robine throws into relief the single most radical break that Gestalt therapy made a half a century ago with western psycho-logical thinking to that point.

Given the elemental place of contact in its theory, what part does the idea of a "self" play in Gestalt therapy? It is essential to distinguish, especially to English speaking readers, what Robine means by the "self" from conventional ways of thinking about it and why he calls it an "unfolding self." The self has long been a centerpiece of Anglo-American psycholog-ical theory, where it has been described as though it shared characteristics with material objects in space (but what kind of space, one might ask, does the self exist in?). The self has thus taken on a questionable definiteness in western psychological thinking, an illusory firmness, as though it were something that could be enclosed in an outline, and then studied, diagnosed, and treated by the therapist, or esteemed, realized, or made authentic by the patient.

Such reified conceptions of the self derive from the Cartesian division of existence into encapsulated individual consciousnesses busy trying to govern an objective material world. In western cultures this split had already been put to use by protestant theologies, especially Calvinist and Puritan ones, which emphasized looking inward (self-scrutiny) and castigating the body. From the secular side, it was subsequently carried forward by nineteenth century positivism. In British and American psychoanalytic schools after Freud, authentic selves, false selves, and core selves sprang up. Even the humanistic psychologies of the mid-twentieth century made the fulfillment of self (self-realization or self-actualization) their goal.

In his nineteen-sixties version of Gestalt therapy, Perls mostly adhered to this individualistic and spatial conception of self. It underpins his vision of layers of false self wrapped around a repressed authentic one waiting to explode into being, and his top dog and underdog, which come across as like pop art versions of the internalizations and identifications of object relations theory. But in Goodman's writings something quite different occurs. In the first part of the theoretical volume of Perls, Hefferline, and Goodman, the self is defined neither from the inside out (as in psychodynamic theories), nor from the outside in (as in behaviorism) but as an aesthetic activity: the activity of shaping experience at that very site where meetings between the person and his or her surrounding environment occur. This is a fascinating suggestion, which defines the self as a temporal process rather than a quasi-spatial entity, and it represents another radical break (although one that Goodman himself by no means maintains consistently) with the prevailing western tradition. It is from this sense of temporal process that Robine takes his cue.

It's not that Robine rejects intrapsychic or other structural views of the psyche out of hand. He knows well enough that they have added considerably to our understanding of human functioning. However he doesn't want the self left there, hanging out to dry, as though suspended in some kind of inner mental space. He is interested in what happens if the theorist follows out Goodman's description of the self as a maker of forms, itself changing form, situated where the organism and the environment engage in constantly changing transactions with one another. Thus put in motion at this edge, the self and its surroundings tend to arise from and dissolve into each other. What is left is a kind of flowing river of momentary, passing forms in which distinctions between self and other, inner and outer, ultimately disappear except as a way of speaking. Robine's conception of self can only be fleetingly and partially grasped as a kind of verb, not by anything so static as a noun. For him, the self is constituted by the passing of time much more than by anything resembling space.

A temporal emphasis does not mean that experience is without structure, but it consists of fluctuating structure in motion. "Gestalt therapy," as Robine puts it, "stems much more from a culture of verbs, or of adverbs, than it does from a culture of nouns. It is not the fixed forms that interest us . . . [here he cites Laura Perls], but the forms in movement, the formation of forms" (p. 10). Robine's vision of the self is rather like a subatomic particle, which can never be pinned down, because it has either already changed or vanished by the time you perceive it and try to name it. Even verbs and adverbs don't quite catch it. With subatomic particles, you only have the sense that they may have been there by the trail they leave behind or because your equations predict that such must be the case. With a temporal self, what is left behind are the forms of experience. These can be frozen in space. A painter paints — and leaves behind his works for us to view. But he has moved on, still painting.

One notices the prevalence of the word "form" in this discussion. Indeed the word appears throughout Robine's work. As in all Gestalt therapy, properly understood, Robine's investigation of experience has always entailed particular attention to how experience is made and thus to the forms one gives to experience in the very act of experiencing ("form" is one of the meanings of the word "Gestalt"). Since the making of form is also a major concern of artists, it is not so surprising as it may seem at first glance that the earliest essay in his previous collection — "An Aesthetic of Psychotherapy" (1984) — looked at Gestalt therapy through the lens of criteria usually reserved for works of art, in contrast to the traditional preoccupation of psychological theory with science (See also Robine Ed. "*La psychotherapie comme esthétique,*" Ed. L'exprimerie: Bordeaux (2006) partly translated in *International Gestalt Journal,* vol. XXX, #1, 2007).

For the therapist, you could say that the aesthetic task is to explore what happens (and what else is possible) when people, in regulating the anxieties of living with uncertainty, staunch the flow of experience and thus design their lives around limited, sometimes severely limited, possibilities. In the language of Gestalt therapy, these are called "fixed Gestalts"; in aesthetic terms, they become stereotypes imposed on experience that cramp it into ill-fitting, inappropriate configurations. This is how Gestalt therapy enters the realm of psychopathology. Robine sees a parallel dangerous tendency in psychological theory itself — to substitute the name or concept itself for what that name or concept momentarily and inadequately points toward. Against this tendency he directs much of his own theorizing. To Robine, the worst sin is to build a theory around names and then claim that such a theory predicts "truths" or give a description of "reality." Such theories, rather than suggestively guiding and supporting the therapist's capacity to improvise, lead to the application of reductive therapeutic formulas to the mysteries of the patient's existence.

The essays in this book illuminate one facet of Gestalt therapy after another from fresh points of view. Despite Robine's taste for the philosophical, there are passages of personal reflection alongside samples drawn from individual and group sessions, so that one comes away from the book with a sense of intimate connection between his development as a theorist and his experience as a therapist. One aspect of this connection in particular merits further discussion here because Robine has drawn upon it for a formulation that may well constitute his most important contribution to the relationship between theory and practice.

Robine's approach to a therapy session is to wait with as few preconceptions as possible and to try to remain open to everything that happens. As figures, shapes, forms, patterns, and roles emerge, the therapist and the patient can scrutinize how these configurations are actually in a process of being put together in the session itself. In the language of postmodernism, one might think of this as a method of experiential deconstruction. Robine treats the therapy session itself as a particular kind of construction, an improvised arrangement in a field of potentials from which an indefinite number of constructions could be made. The aim is to heighten awareness of possibilities (besides the usually fixed, symptomatic one that the patient brings in) in the ongoing stream of experience as it forms. From this vantage point the theorist can investigate, and the therapist can experiment with, how patient and therapist together actively and collaboratively go about giving structure and meaning to the present *situation*, a word that he borrows from Goodman, and which Goodman took over from John Dewey. In the case of a therapy session, the situation might be described as this room in which these two people — this patient and this therapist — sit down together and begin to speak (no doubt innumerable other descriptions are possible). The situation, understood in this way, is a wide-open arena, with nothing taken for granted, ripe for collaborative creative exploration and experimentation. For Robine, phenomenological innocence, the bracketing of assumptions, is the point of departure, one that has its roots planted firmly in the classical theory of Gestalt therapy.

Taking the situation, an everyday word, as a fundamental theoretical concept for psychotherapy may seem, at first glance, too simple an idea for a discipline traditionally given to arcane terminology. As Robine uses it, in fact, it is a concept of considerable power and complexity, arrived at in his recent writing through a developmental trajectory that runs throughout these essays. To understand its full import, one needs to see how it is related to the traditional place of field theory in Gestalt therapy.

Since Gestalt therapy conceives of human experience as a sequence of transitory constructions, the question naturally arises, from what raw material is experience made, if one is not to end up with a claim that it is made *ex nihilo*? (To make such a claim would confuse the phenomenological basis of Gestalt therapy with an extreme relativism that says nothing exists except our fabrications. Neither Goodman's text nor Robine's postmodern reworking of it would settle for this sort of solipsistic or nihilistic position.) Perls and Goodman assumed that what exists before experience was the "organism/environment field," an undifferentiated landscape of potentialities that precedes every human encounter, every appearance of the self, every separation into categories or entities (such as self and other). The idea that a primitive condition of unity is the prerequisite for division into organism and environment filtered into Gestalt therapy from a number of sources — among them, the holistic theories of J. C. Smuts and Kurt Goldstein (both of whom deeply influenced Perls), the interactionist social psychology of Dewey, and the social science field theory of the Gestalt psychologist Kurt Lewin. To the extent that field theory has provided a framework for much of the thinking about Gestalt therapy during the past dozen years or so, it has helped in turning recent theory away from Perls's later individualistic bias toward a more relational and ecological emphasis.

However, the organism/environment field, perhaps too much ploughed over, has begun to show signs of fatigue. It seems headed for a fate like that which befell the "self" — of becoming abstract and reified. In part this is due to Kurt Lewin's influence. Lewin was a physicist before he turned to social science and psychology. He derived his ideas from the electromagnetic and quantum field theories, which attempted to account for the impact of the whole on the part and the part on the whole, even across such distances that it can be far from obvious how parts and wholes are related to each other. Field theory has revolutionized physics, but it represents a high order of abstraction, especially when applied to human behavior. Thus much of recent Gestalt therapy field theory has tended to replace the drama of particulars that make up human experience with grand abstractions that seem remote from what psychotherapists actually do.

In his own writings, Robine has often tackled the question of the organism/environment conception of field theory. Several of the essays here address it, although with increasing dissatisfaction about its Lewinian leaning toward abstraction, as well as its tendency, despite its holistic premises, toward giving too much credibility once again to the individual organism, which can drift back into what Robine calls a "one-person psychology." (It seems incredibly difficult to keep psychological theory from slipping into this single-minded focus on the encapsulated individual — a difficulty that probably stems not from human nature but from the conditioning of the western mind.) So in characteristic fashion he returned recently to Perls's and Goodman's text and found there a series of hints about the "situation," which he elaborated into alternative, more concrete way of describing the psychotherapy session as a special kind of two-person field.

Robine gives a lovely example of how the Gestalt therapist pays attention to the way in which one contacts one's world as the elemental psychological fact that underlies all one's shaping of experience, including that of relationships. He tells of "the patient who complained to me of being invaded and overwhelmed by her relational environment, which intruded on her life and demanded ever more of her. As she was speaking to me, she seemed unaware of a brilliant ray of sunshine which was striking her face and blinding her: she would only have needed to shift her chair a few centimeters to regain some minimal degree of comfort." The example also illustrates perfectly how a therapist might make use of what is available in the present situation.

This transformation of the "field" into a specifically therapeutic "situation" is an impressive accomplishment, because it re-grounds field theory phenomenologically in the actual practice of psychotherapy. It is also a difference in theoretical focal length, like the difference between a geological map and a photograph of a local neighborhood. Both are useful, depending on what you are looking for. But it seems to me that the photograph is far more useful to the psychotherapist and to the student of human nature as well. Without sailing off into cosmic abstraction or sinking back into an individualistic model, Robine manages to build a theory that restores the therapy session as a stage for the idiosyncratic, unpredictable drama of human existence.

PART 1

INTRODUCTION TO PART 1

The chapters in Part 1 were written over a period of five years. Some of the slightly earlier work published in my previous book (*Gestalt thérapie, la construction du soi*, Harmattan) already contained the seeds of the change that occurred during this time, but it is the writings presented here which contain what I experienced as a radical transformation. However, writing, both before and after this, remains for me an act of contact. My writing is constantly transformed by contact with my patients, my students and my colleagues; their contributions have revealed my theoretical shortcomings and stimulated me to further search; meeting other researchers, reading their publications has provided illumination in dark areas; our conversations sketched out the form of subsequent writing. I have never been able to write down fixed ideas. Fixed ideas are dead, and the white page can only be their shroud.

I have therefore kept the chapters in chronological order as this shows the process of their development. This process was one of rebounds, retracings, forward surges and then re-roots, hesitations and repetitions, spirals and sometimes dark labyrinths, seeking an engagement, an engaged uncertainty, the curiosity which makes one take a step forward into uncertain territory. "Faith is knowing, beyond awareness, that if one takes a step there will be ground underfoot" (Perls, Hefferline, & Goodman, 1994). He returned to this idea in his last work (*Little Prayers and Finite Experience*, 1972) "The next moment is not the edge of the precipice. Thanks to faith, I am not a prisoner in the finite cage of my own experience: it has a horizon, not bars."

Trying to entrench the move from an individualistic approach to a field or situational approach means asking psychotherapy to make a kind of "quantum leap." It involves rupture and tearing away, the abandonment of loyalties with a thousand years of so-called evidence behind them. However, it is increasingly clear to me that the field perspective does not need to be opposed to an intra-psychological one, rather it can include it. But this dialectic entails a certain rigor — not always easy to maintain, as some of the illustrations in the second part will demonstrate — which transforms the very foundations of the individualist approach. We have to forge new concepts and redefine others, and above all continue to make choices in how we think, that is to say, insofar as possible, to avoid being thought by our thoughts, or as Maldiney puts it so well, to emerge from the "self-which-is-done-to."

1

WILL GESTALT THERAPY DARE TO ENTER

A POSTMODERN WAY?*

What I propose to explore here, under this somewhat mysterious title, are some of the lines of force and paradigms which run implicitly or explicitly through the theory of Gestalt therapy, with the idea of drawing a certain number of consequences for clinical practice. I believe that if we can better understand these lines of force, we will be able to apply them better, and at the same time more easily understand the lines of fracture which divide those who promote Gestalt therapy. I also want to stress at the outset that I am not entirely happy to be relying on this term "postmodernism," which is far too

---

* Translated by Gordon Wheeler. Published in *Studies in Gestalt Therapy* Istituto di Gestalt-HCC, Italy, vol. 8, 1999. Originally published in French in *Cahiers de Gestalt-thérapie*, nº 5, 1999.

charged with a variety of connotations; but I will make use of it all the same, for want of a better one, while trying to specify what I see as the shape and limits of the concept.

Some people, the minute they hear terms like "episte-mology," fear the worst — what Perls termed, in his colorful language, "mind-fucking" — which is to say, "massaging the gray matter," or "mental masturbation." I hope to avoid this risk, particularly since the material I want to take up here is highly charged for me emotionally, so that my theoretical re-flections here arise out of my own personal development, and out of clinical practice and theory as well. In a previous study, I opened with a citation from Prinzhorn (1984), taken from his work about "Gestaltung": "We look for the meaning of each formed form in the act of formation itself," which is to say that in the questions that concern us here, the meaning of the form which I will arrive at, the conclusions and above all the ques-tions, can be sought in my own process and development, the-oretical and clinical practice as well, which I will thus turn to now.

FRAGMENTS OF AN ITINERARY

At the beginning of the 80s, after having been trained and having practiced Gestalt therapy for some time — at first in a Perlsian form (from the Esalen period), then modified by the contribution of the Gestalt Institute of Cleveland (in par-ticular the Polsters) — I had the opportunity to work for several years with Isadore From, a member of Gestalt therapy's founding group. This led me to a reexamination, painful and radical, led me to turn my back firmly on certain practices, certain theoretical notions, and a certain ethic, in favor of another approach, that of Goodman and From, which I saw from the beginning as more demanding (and I was still far from appreciating all its implications). At the time it was difficult for me to distinguish the contribution of From from that of Goodman, and all the more so since during the course of my two previous Gestalt trainings, I had never even heard either name mentioned.

As much as I had the impression (rightly or wrongly) of having rapidly assimilated the Perlsian and Cleveland models, to the point of reaching their limits and recognizing their impasses in my first months of practice, just as much do I have the impression now, after nearly two decades, of not yet having completed the full tour of the model proposed by Goodman. I would say with some distance on it now that it took me six to eight years to get past "introjection," only partly chewed to the point of assimilation, then several years more to be able to challenge certain points, and to move beyond what these masters gave me, and pursue new paths that they had opened up. (At the same time, I am far from considering that the model transmitted to us by Goodman is in any way perfect! I only mean to say that new paths are opened up, which it is up to us to identify and then explore.)

Thus it took me some years to detach myself from the restrictions of an approach based on Goodman's work, as applied by From — while realizing at the same time that my own reading constitutes another form of restriction in itself. The restriction which I am referring to is of a structural order: the approach to the self which From constructed rested heavily on one of the aspects of the self in Perls and Goodman — namely, the partial structures, the three functions, their disturbances and losses, and so on. This at least is my perception of From's teaching, which was probably less true of his practice, which was more process-oriented in nature (even though he rejected the word "process" as not a phenomenological term).

From my reading of Goodman was then born my preoccupation with the field. Of course, I had always heard of "the field." It was always a concept which floated through the discourse of Gestaltists, without ever quite being pinned down or actually taken account of, beyond the level of slogans and ritual nods. Once I actually began to reflect, to work, and to explore in this area, I became alarmed. A veritable vertigo set in, in the face of the challenges I anticipated. The loss of certainties painfully acquired, and all the more so, given that it had never been easy to identify oneself as a Gestalt therapist in the first place, in the world of establishment psychology which I had long been a part of. But at least the structural reference points which I could call on at the time did locate me in a way of thinking that was relatively banalized, institutionalized, and to all appearances shared by an immense majority of colleagues. I imagined that serious reliance on field concepts would isolate me even further, leaving me to forge on alone, which seemed to me — and still seems — both impossible and unimaginable.

In a 1989 paper, "Field Neurosis," which was a lecture given at a research meeting devoted to "Transference in Gestalt Therapy," I wrote the following: "One thing is certain to me as I write these lines: I am frightened! I anticipate that my compelling yet disordered reflections of recent times, if I push them to their radical limits, could lead me to such an epistemological rupture that I would be even more alone, permanently isolated from those who have constructed a comfortable status quo, at the far edges of what can continue to be read and accepted. Will I have this courage?"

A second personal path, seemingly unrelated but in fact deeply connected to the first theme, was broached for me by my work with shame.

In 1991, at the time that I published a first and far too theoretical study on shame, to my knowledge nothing or almost nothing had been published in French on this subject, and not only in Gestalt therapy. Since that time studies have flourished, including in the Gestalt world, at least in the English language. Why shame? The more I deepened my work with borderline and narcissistic personality disorders, the more the question of shame presented itself, indirectly. Never, in my personal therapies or my supervision, had I encountered this theme; and certainly I was permeated with it without knowing it. My own shame, non-conscious and not worked through, took such form as it could take, when such dynamics are not taken account of: that is, I projected it. I dealt in shame without realizing it; I attempted to escape it by generating it in others, which then allowed me to take care of my old narcissistic wounds — or rather, to bury them with illusions . . . and did not insist on the therapeutic relevance of the theme, in spite of the difficulties, in the relationship with my patients. The shame I am speaking of is beyond its immediately felt form, in certain embarrassing situations, beyond the possibility of creating a reaction formation as well, lying more in the realm of the right to existence itself — in the recognition that I receive, or do not receive, in being what I am, feeling what I feel, desiring as I desire. Thus I have been able to discover that each time I am in a situation which causes me to feel that I should be somehow other than I am, I am in a situation of shame. You can imagine then the degree to which it is easy for a therapist, a supervisor, a trainer, to place whomever he is working with in a position of shame, by giving him the implicit message that he ought to be other than he is, and all the more so, in view of the fact that this client, this trainee or supervisee is coming there precisely because he does consider that he should indeed be other than he is.

Out of this concern, and the work which it led me to do on this theme (will it ever be completed?), the importance of the question of support also became more clear to me. To be sure, just as for every Gestaltist, the "enemy twins" of support and frustration were part of the methodological equipment offered by Perls. But it is also true that when I read or watch the session protocols he left for posterity, I find more there to nourish my competence in providing frustration than I do for providing support. Even Laura Perls, who provided a counter-weight to her husband in the application of these "enemy twins," by giving support to support, shared only a few thoughts on this subject. Still, I had long realized my own irritation at Perls's proposal that therapy would mean the transition from environmental support to self-support — a proposition that I had and still have a hard time distinguishing from an invitation to egotism. Nonetheless — and working with shame confronts us directly with this point — support begins with the reception and recognition of that which is present in the experience of contact at the boundary, which is to say, with that which is, such as it is, and not such as I might wish it were.

It is also true — and this is directly connected with my personal history — that my previous reluctance to open myself to giving or receiving support was related to an intrusion anxiety, the fear of being the victim or the agent of intrusion — as well as anxieties about dependence, again both depending on others and being depended on. The context of these fears includes all the mythology of autonomy and responsibility developed in our own field of the human sciences, both clinical and social, particularly through this past century, as will be discussed further below.

Today, these fears are no longer so strong as they may have been some years ago: the context has changed, and thus I have learned to seek out and accept various forms of support. No doubt the serious automobile accident which I was involved in around a year before this writing, confronting me as it did with the imminent probability of my own death, contributed as well to modifying my views and my contact with my world, in such a way that I no longer experience these fears in the same way. Certain retroflections have vanished — or else been reestablished someplace else!

There you have some fundamental dynamics of my personal and professional evolution of recent years. I have taken some pains to sketch them here because the figures which I want to develop now have a ground, personally as well as theoretically — and also because theory-building itself is necessarily a matter of trying to construct meaning out of one's own experience, and perhaps integrating that experience into a larger order of generalization.

The theoretical developments which I wish to trace with you here arise first and foremost out of myself, and must be closely examined in those terms, if they are to lay claim to generalization in this way. If something of all this is able to resonate with your own experience, and serve to help you in ordering that experience meaningfully, I will not have wasted my time.

A Re-reading of *Gestalt Therapy* by Perls and Goodman at a Distance of Half a Century

Once one has gained a certain familiarity with our founding text, with the passage time particular "discomfort zones" may begin to come to light. Certain contradictions may well appear, then disappear, only to reappear further along, in particular with regard to the conception of self. The advances of thinking in contemporary social sciences, philosophy, sociology, even the history of art, help us to identify certain apparent contradictions, to explain them, and in that way to try to get beyond them. These critical perspectives, it seems to me, can be found in the passage from "modernity" to what is now conveniently called "postmodernity."

Modernity corresponds to that modality of thinking which, since the Enlightenment, has sought o open new vistas of scientific and technical progress, as well as new areas of knowledge which represent a break with the more or less obscurantist traditions of previous centuries. On the social level, for all that the various thinkers, sociologists, and social critics may diverge in their analyses, they are all in agreement in connecting "modernity" with the arise of the primacy of the individual, and its "perverse effect": individualism itself.

Indeed, modernity is associated with the rise of reason and science, of the "Rights of Man," along with the principles of equality and liberty, of the destruction of the social fabric of tribal community in favor of the concept of "society," and thus the primacy of individuality and the idea of the subject, which are so central to contemporary social science. Thus it is modernity which has given rise to Romanticism, and with it the notion of the emotions as preeminent. The aesthetic attitude thereby replaces the religious.

From this point, everything is then in place for fostering interest in adjustment in and by means of contact, creativity, and autonomy and responsibility, all of them so closely linked to the definition itself of "the subject."

The years 1950-1970 seem to me today to represent the peak of what is commonly called modernity; and *Gestalt Ther apy*, published in 1951, contains numerous references to this mode of thinking: the idea of approaching "the self" through its partial structures, the emphasis on responsibility, the autonomy of the subject, the references to psychopathology, the support drawn (albeit critically) from making reference to Freudian and Reichian ideas, the often unclear distinction between the self and the "ego" or "I" (or the organism), and so on. All these references to modernity were then further amplified in the later work of Perls, but not that of Goodman — which does show clearly which of the two men exerted more influence on their joint project in the direction of modernist ideas.

But at the same time, Perls and Goodman introduced a fundamental shift which places them at the very heart of what would later be called "postmodernity": they displaced the self, relocated it, decentralized it, and temporalized it (that is, they took away the notion of its timeless or ideal nature). In the modernist approach, the individual self was recognized, solipsistically, as the sole reality. By contrast, Goodman, whose influence it was that took the theory in this direction, put forward the idea that the self is contact. But quite often, the gestaltist self is then reduced to the notion of organism, or one of its equivalents (the "ego," the subject, the person) — because it is unacceptable to think of oneself other than as something that has continuity? And yet Goodman and Perls do specify unambiguously: "The self is only a small factor in the total organism/environment interaction, but it plays the crucial role which consists in developing and creating the meanings by which we are able to develop" (Perls et al., 1951).

Goodman makes reference to a primary reality: that which exists, is the field. Once the field is then defined as "an organism and its environment," the self then delineates the internal movements of the field, movements of integration and differentiation, unification and individuation, action and transformation, and so on.

But this opening expressed by Perls and Goodman is not always respected, neither by themselves, nor, as is to be expected, by their followers. Can one respect it? Are we not easily tempted to revert to the individualist or solipsist paradigm, which we chose to call "organism," "psyche," "person," patient or client? Are we not then easily tempted to contribute to the development of the psychopathology of an isolated entity, even if that psychopathology leads to further problematics, such as Heidegger's "being-in-the-world"? Are we not tempted to make reference to a kind of psychogenesis — even when, as is more and more common these days, that psychogenesis takes some account of early relations with the environment, or "object relations," at the risk of reducing the environment in general, and the other person with it, to an instrumental or pragmatic role, the "cause" of development and its disturbances? Let us return to an example which I was citing earlier: Perls, in his last period, emphasized the notion of "self-support." This he opposed to "environmental support." One can see clearly here the opposition between self and environment, at the same point where we would have found "organism" and "environment," in his joint work with Goodman. Thus if we superimpose "self" on "person" or "organism," we arrive at the positing of all kinds of individual capacities and self-resources, from a position of egotism.

If on the other hand we consider the self as contact itself, we will rather promote the discovery of support in the contact within the field (remembering that the field includes both organism and environment). The unavoidable conclusion is that we are confronted with two quite different psychotherapies. Can we then call two such different psychotherapies by the same name, "Gestalt therapy"?

Rather than launching reproaches at our primary Gestalt authors, we may consider these different and contradictory aspects as symptoms of the characteristic modernist/postmodernist oscillation of the times. Quite the contrary, they seem to me to have been able to make room in their own thinking for a significant step beyond the common discourse of their times and context. It is up to us, with our contemporary tools of analysis, to find the way to move beyond certain unclarities or inconsistencies in their work.

A Digression
Into the Question of "Postmodernism"

Postmodernism, it seems to me, is far from a homogeneous movement, for all that it may be relatively coherent in the hands of one or another of its theoreticians. To go more deeply into the question than this, it would be necessary to cite the contradictions among the different domains which lay claim to this label. For example, postmodernism in music uses parameters which are sharply different from, even contradictory, to those of architecture, which are themselves different from those of the art media. If one then includes the dynamics of meaning suggested by philosophy, sociology, epistemology and other disciplines, one could rapidly lose one's bearings entirely. With postmodernity arises, in the felicitous phrase of Max Weber, the "desire for the reenchantment of the world." The forms may at times be chaotic, but the notion of chaos itself, with all the doubts and tensions associated with it, is an integral part of the postmodern paradigm. Many of these domains are the object of a "de-" plus another term: deconstruction, decomposition, decentralization, deregulation, desacralization, disinformation . . . The postmodern signals the loss of illusions — of progress, of science, of truth, and the hegemony of the dominant culture.

In psychology, it is customary to include under postmodernism (or more precisely, under one of its branches, constructivism): Gestalt theory, the work of Piaget, and the works of the Palo Alto School. In both psychology and psychotherapy, postmodernism is ushered in under a sort of double impulsion: on the one hand the influence of the constructivist movement, including certain work at the very heart of the psychoanalytic movement, such as that of Viderman (1970), as well as the opposition which has been opened up between discovery and construction; and on the other hand the dialogic movement initiated by Buber and furthered by Levinas, Ricoeur, and others, along with those movements known as interactionist, inter-subjective, conversational, and other variants on the primacy of otherness and relationship (or in the field, as we might rather say), in the definition of humanness itself.

I would particularly cite the impact of constructivist thinking as one of the active currents of this kind of postmodernism. With constructivism comes the awareness that there is no reality other than that which we construct — which sweeps away the myth of objectivity in science, and in all the other approaches, including those of the human or social sciences, which flirt with the scientific method.

Modernism rests on the premise which could be expressed in the old adage, "I only believe what I see." Post-modernism would rather say, "I only see what I believe."

With social constructionism, a line of thinking drawn from constructivism by Berger and Luckmann (1966), and developed by Gergen (1991, 1994) and others, the emphasis is further elaborated in a direction which unites both of the two postmodernist strands which I was discussing above: there is no other reality than that which we construct *in relationship*.

This hypothesis is not without consequences for the psychotherapist's stance in the field of his or her relationship with his/her patients. We find ourselves implicated in a co-construction of meaning on the basis of what is experienced in the relationship of the words which give form to that experience even as they are embodied by that experience itself.

Under the influence of philosophers like Wittgenstein, Ricoeur, Lyotard, Gadamer (to cite only some of the most influential), the accent here is on language. "The limits of our language furnish the limits of our world," wrote Wittgenstein in 1953 — by which he meant that the limits of the structures of our telling, the terms which we hold and hold out to others, our capacity to express ourselves in words, will define our possibilities for understanding and explaining, and will trace the outlines of what we will call "reality." In other words, the words we use and the accounts which we construct for understanding our experience constitute what can be included or excluded in that experience.

From there, everything that we say about the notions of identity and "self" will be informed by the postmodern wave. In the traditional conception, whether romantic or modern, the self is inseparable from continuity, the deepening of inferiority. "Normal" and "pathological" are more or less linked to a person's capacity to be in touch with his/her identity at the deepest level; and therapy — particularly those therapies which are called "modern" — has the goal of enabling the subject to accede to this condition.

In the postmodern perspective, the accent is on the evolution of contexts, and a concern for the establishment of perspectives will replace the fascination with personal history, while the question of how changes may occur will predominate over the "why" of the various meanings which come to light. In this view we are the product of the contexts of our conversations, and of meanings which we derive socially. And in as much as our conversations are constantly changing, our "selves" are in perpetual movement, and ultimately as multiple as our situations.

As Epstein (1995) remarks, this mutation of vocabulary, from one which described an object called "self" to one which describes the self as a product of an endlessly variable social interaction, requires a radical change in psychology, and thus in psychotherapy. The problem is no longer to be or not to be in true "contact" with who we "really are," our most profound identity — but rather to recover flexibility in our fictions, our discourse, our histories, our narratives, and the myths which we use every day in telling these things, to ourselves and others.

With this perspective we lose the certainty that we "have" riches within, in our deepest inner being, which are latent or exploited to a greater or lesser degree. And along with that we lose the basic support for the notion of the unconscious. We lose as well the fictions of identity, and along with this, the possibility of an objective, measurable knowledge of the other person.

We also lose standards for "normality," and with it the need to know a "truth," which would be understood as other than another fiction. Lost as well, is the concern for measuring, diagnosing, and other techniques which derive from the idea of norms. We lose interest in historical, decontextualized explanations. In the clinical and therapeutic relationship, we lose the position of power and domination which goes with being the one who knows, or is assumed to know — and our patients lose the shame of not knowing, and of being controlled without knowing it by hidden forces and unseen truths.

Each of us can decide for him or herself whether these losses are to be celebrated or deplored!

And what does the postmodern perspective offer us, in exchange for all this?

We gain the conviction that every theory is a fiction among other fictions, but that it is through and by means of those fictions that we try to construct meaning out of our experience. Since the emphasis is now on the co-construction of meanings in relationship, we assign a new and central importance to conversational situations, and thus to relationship, connection, bonding, and community, as opposed to the accent in the individualist paradigm on the terms of autonomy and personal responsibility. If we lose independence, we gain interdependence. We are now focused on the "how" of experiences, much more than on their "why," on the creative invention of the adjustment or solution, far more than on causal explanation. "Here, now, and next," as opposed to "here and now, because back then . . . " Therapy itself then becomes the cocreation of a context, and no longer talks about a given frame. (And in this regard it is interesting to note that where the English term is "setting," literally a placing or positioning, in French we use the equivalent of "frame." There too we can see how our words are loaded with fictions.) The flexibility of the self, generally approached in terms of process, becomes more the focus than the search for a "true self" which one should attain, and thus fix in position. Psychotherapy becomes an activity which is not only a matter of language, but is a new experience based on two distinct experiences, expressed in distinct words, in which the conflict of these fictions or representations, as well as the fusion of these multiple horizons, permits the construction of new meanings. And thus the therapist is invited to position her/himself as curious, naive, and dialogically exposed to the subjectivity of the other person, and not to take up an expert presence.

There too, it is up to each of us to determine whether this conception represents the possibility of a step forward, or of a loss.

An Alternative for Gestalt Therapy

Thus in our founding text we are confronted with two paradigms, which may appear resolutely contradictory: on the one hand the individualist model, in which the self is taken as fundamentally separate, the model which gives us the line of thinking we call "intrapsychic"; and on the other hand the paradigm of the field as the "primary motor" (to steal a phrase from Aristotle), a model which privileges contact and relationship. On the one hand the model of oral aggression proposed by Perls, and on the other that of creative adjustment developed by Goodman. In the one perspective the subject is primary; in the other, the field.

Among Gestaltists, Gordon Wheeler is without a doubt one of those who has taken his own thinking the farthest in this domain (1996); but we find a similar perspective, in different terms to be sure, in the work of Lee McLeod (1995), in the recent writings of Gary Yontef (1993), and even in Joel Latner, in his article "This is the Speed of Light: Field Theory and Systems Theory" (1983), which was unsatisfying in various respects but nonetheless a pioneering effort.

In one of his recent articles (1996), Wheeler offers a schematic comparison of the two paradigms which are at the heart of our debate today. Let us examine his presentation of the individualist paradigm (Table 1):

Table 1: The perspective of the individual paradigm

self	preexistent before relationship, fundamentally separate, unconnected by its nature with the environment or other selves
other	separate from self; the object of self-energy, to be made use of or exploited fundamentally competitive with self
human nature	the discharge of drives; self-process in isolation from the field
relationship	not primary; secondary to self existence; subject-object or object-object by nature
observer position	outside the person or system observed, fundamentally separate, mutually uninfluenced; expert model
process	taking in of nourishment, discharge of tension

development	self does not develop; only the object map develops
community	source of constraints on self-expression
therapy	to correct deficiencies/distortions in object map; to promote adjustment and compromise between natural drives and social constraints
view of reality	positivist; reality is given before self or perception
criteria of knowledge	scientific or objective confirmation; authority-based
right	wrong emphasis
nature of authority	hierarchical, authoritarian; "right-wrong," expert approach
nature of power	authoritarian and dominant, by the very terms of human nature; benevolent or abusive coercion, "discipline" model
criteria of health	maximum self-expression consistent with self-preservation
direction of development	from infantile dependency to mature adult autonomy
understanding of shame	social vulnerability; results from excessive dependency on others; the immature form of guilt
psychotherapy	focused on inner process, aimed at strengthening autonomy

To deepen the differentiation, Wheeler then places the two paradigms in perspective: the field paradigm and the individualist paradigm, in the following table:

Table 2

	Individualist Paradigm	Field/Gestalt paradigm
self	preexistent, separate precedes relationship	the integration of "inner" and "outer" experience, includes relationship
other	separate from self, object of self-drives	fundamentally connected as coequal pole of self-experience
human nature	discharge of drives, isolated from field	meaningful self-organization of experience, the construction of meaning as primary drive
relationship	secondary, subject-object or object-object	primary, subject-subject
boundary	separates self from field	joins "me" to "other," locus of self process: bounds of self-process
observer position	objectivist perspective, experience seen from the outside	phenomenological perspective, experience seen from outside the other's experience seen from inside

process	tension discharge	organization of the field of experience in relation to external conditions, internal needs and goals
development	progression of object choices	evolution of self-process toward more and more inclusive/integrated
community	opposed to individual	coequal with individual as dynamic pole of self experience
therapy	removing blocks/distortions to tension discharge	support of a more robust self-to tension discharge process, through intersubjective contact
view of reality	positivist/objectivist	constructivist/phenomenological
criteria of knowledge	scientific/objective	dialogic constructivism, "reality" as process confirmation, "reality" precedes perception and subjectivity
nature of authority	hierarchical, expert "right-wrong" orientation	consensual/dialogic process
power	authoritarian, one-way	shared, collaborative
health	maximum self-expression	ongoing process of greater wholes of meaning
direction of development	from infantile dependency to mature adult autonomy	from narrower to wider fields of experience, interdependent with field

shame	infantile form of guilt, sign of immature field dependency	modulating affect in contact, sign of lack of support in the field

If I do agree with Wheeler's theses through a large part of their development, I would make a distinction on one point in particular. Wheeler assimilated the field paradigm to the constructivist approach. It is true that it is the logic of the constructivism which allows us to enter this new paradigm on a firm footing, and with much greater clarity than was offered by phenomenology or Gestalt psychology, as precursor elements. But in spite of that, to my way of thinking at least, constructivism itself remains locked in the individualist paradigm: its "there is no other reality than that which each subject constructs," rests on an affirmation of solipsism. It is the movement to social constructionism which changes this dictum, into, again, "there is no other reality than that which each subject constructs *in relationship*." This is the true sign, to my thinking, of the paradigmatic shift.

Let us then touch on certain paths for a development of the theory and practice of Gestalt therapy in these directions:

a) The importance of the construction of narrative

All the various work which derives from this way of thinking invites us to take an interest in the construction of narrative. In the United States, where the impact of postmodernism is much more marked than in France, this interest in narration has already given rise to new schools of therapy, such as "Narrative therapy." Erv Polster himself, some seven or eight years ago, published a book called *Every Person's Life is Worth a Novel* (1987). But the capacity to construct a narrative on the basis of one's experience was already touched on directly by Goodman in *Gestalt Therapy*, with his evocation of "rhetorical attitudes." While this was only sketched out in a relatively minimal way, he did show how these attitudes act on the formation of personality, and are constructed in interpersonal relationships, both in verbal content, and perhaps even more in the nonverbal (voice, syntax, the way of expressing oneself, and so on).

But the fact itself that Goodman opens this path in connection with his discussion of the formation of personality and the personality function of the self, should draw our attention: personality is only one aspect, one modality of self. Self cannot be reduced and restricted to what we call personality, as Polster unfortunately does, in my opinion, all through his writings.

That Winnicott, Jung, or others also offer a conception of self which is close to what we in the Gestalt model call personality, is not so problematic, to my way of thinking, because with these other writers we are in an entirely different frame of reference.

But the richness, the genius of Perls and Goodman lies in their offering us a construct, the self, which adds and integrates, among other things, both the "id function" (which is to say, the given situation as the mobilization of a direction of desire and meaning), and the "ego function" (which is the capacity to orient the contact with the world, and thus to construct experience).

Keeping this much in mind can help us develop our work on the personality function, by means of narrative studies. But it should not lead us to take the part for the whole, by confusing work on personality with the restoration of self.

b) Revisiting field theory

More often evoked as a slogan than as a methodological reality, field theory in Gestalt therapy, regrounded in a return to the basic principles of Lewin (1938, 1952, 1959), enables us to enter the "social construction of reality" envisioned by postmodernism, on a firmer footing.

The field, or lifespace, is defined by Lewin as the total psychological environment of which a person has subjective experience. From this he derives five essential principles (as quoted by Parlett, 1991, 1993):

1) the principle of organization: behavior is derived from the totality of coexistent facts. The meaning of an "isolated fact" depends on its position in the field.

2) the principle of contemporaneity: it is present dynamics which are explanatory. There is no particular past cause or future objective which is to be considered.

3) the principle of singularity: each situation is unique; circumstances differ, and generalizations are suspect.

4) the principle of variable process: experience is provisional, not permanent.

5) principle of possible relevancy: nothing in the field can be excluded a priori as irrelevant, even if it appears tangential.

On the basis of these principles, field theory enables us to examine the state and operational modalities between the whole and the parts of the field, which is to say, to consider how the parts affect the whole, and how the whole affects the parts. With this orientation we have the possibility of avoiding the syncretic risk contained in the holographic paradigm (the risk of seemingly having to account for everything in order to account for anything) — or, to take a formulation offered by my colleague Jacques Blaize and myself, the possibility of approaching experience as metonomy, the part which may represent the whole without being the whole (as opposed to a systematic approach through metaphor, which is the generalizing tendency of perspectives organized around transference).

At the same time, it will also be necessary to reconsider a number of our definitions, often too implicit, so as to delineate our concepts more clearly in a field perspective. I am thinking in particular of the self-functions outlined by Goodman, "id," "ego," and "personality," which all too often are treated as intrapsychic structures, when actually they would gain in usefulness, in my view, by being considered as functions of the field. The "id," that is, defined from a biological point of view as impulse, or as given by the situation. The "personality" as a registration of field events, and as a here-and-now mobilization, again as a function of the parameters of the situation. And the "ego," that which identifies and alienates: could it possibly do this outside of a context, an environment?

I am thinking too of boundary phenomena such as introjection, retroflection, and so on. Can we introject if there is not an other to "spoon-feed" us? Retroflect, if there is no other person to incite us, with greater or lesser compliance on our part? And so on.

Psychotherapy is thus to be thought of first and foremost as an intersection: the field between.

c) Temporality

In contrast to traditional modes of thinking which "localize" the psyche (even if only metaphorically), and which make an icon of the concept of "topos" (or Aristotle's generalizable rules of placement, which hold outside of time), the theoretical system of Gestalt therapy gives primacy to process and temporality, favoring "chronos" or the dimension of ongoing time, over "topes," or place, which is timeless. Remember that "topic," in the sense of thematic rules, derives from topography or place. This term serves to designate the point of view, in metapsychology, which locates psychic processes as "places" in psychic geography. To be sure, this terminology is also a fiction, and to be distinguished from a "topological" approach, or the "topological psychology" of Kurt Lewin (*op. cit.*), who borrowed his descriptive field model from field theory in physics and from topological mathematics. Between "topical" and "topological" there is the same distinction as between "chronical" (or chronicle) and "chronology." Chronology aims at establishing order in the dates and events of history, while "chronicle" refers above all to narration, real or imaginary, which attempts to reflect social or historical "reality," as given by temporal order. Some fifteen years ago I wrote of the importance of "caraways," which designates a precise instant and helps us understand our famous "here and now." What is important here is that with chronos we understand the duration of time, and through that, process, sequences, and cycles.

A central reference point of Gestalt therapy, then, is the "chronicle" as opposed to the "topical" (central, not exclusive). The chronicle is the forming of forms, the "chronicle" of experience, of the organization of meaning, of the field of consciousness, of contacts, of the construction of contact in relationship and interpersonal connection. This is because in our experience the self cannot be "localized" in the same way: for example, in full action or "full contact," the self is not experienced in the same way as in an integration phase of assimilation, withdrawal, rest, meditation, or preparation for new contacting.

I will not elaborate further on this dimension here, other than to insist on the necessity of completing the western localizing modality of thinking in spatial terms (superficial/deep, center, beneath, behind, foreground/background, internal life, etc.), with a reference to time. Only a reference to temporality, in my opinion, can enable us to surmount the paradox contained in the diverse definitions of self advanced by Perls and Goodman. The end of Chapter VIII of their work (1951) reminds us of this forcefully.

This reference to temporality, associated with the field paradigm and to be understood in the sense of "chronicle," should permit us to resist the siren call which lurks for every navigator of our type: that of developmentalism, biographical causality, and a psychopathology founded on fixations or regressions in the developmental stages of the "libido" or in object relations. We might reread the highly instructive pages which Lewin (op. cit.) devoted to the idea of regression. If we do not put temporality in this restricted sense of historicism and etiology at the center of our concerns, then I believe that we can be more open to considerations of the level of dynamic, interpersonal and social processes which sustain symptoms and suffering.

d) From contact to relationship

I have always disagreed with the amalgamation, on the part of many Gestaltists, of "contact" and "relationship." The essential part of *Gestalt Therapy* speaks of contact, and very little of relationship. To be sure, contact is a component of relationship, a part of a more complex whole. The elaborations proposed by Perls and Goodman with regard to contact are not transferable to the notion of relationship. The theoretical pathways to relationship are still open, and will long remain so.

At the end of the 1980s, I attempted to approach this concept of contact theoretically, and to define it independently of relationship (Robine, 1991). The field gave little support for this attempt at that time, and I felt the need to submit my study, with considerable anxiety, to Isadore From, whose habit it was never, or almost never, to make any commentary in reply. In this case he agreed to do so, and we spoke at great length about this article, which he approved of, which did give me considerable reassurance.

Today I am most aware of the limits of this text, and the work which remains to move ahead with the articulation of the contact/relationship distinction. The question of what is therapeutic, in the therapeutic relationship, among others, is one which impels us to push ahead on this path, now that we can no longer answer that question monolithically, by appealing to the manipulation of transference. How we should conceive the therapeutic relationship, given the tools that we have, in a way that is coherent with our theory of self, is one of the important questions to be taken up now in the ongoing articulation of Gestalt therapy theory.

At the same time, in raising this question of relationship, I would like to open a political parenthesis here as well. At a time when the community at large is concerned to endow the psychotherapist with a specific definition and status, to define self in terms of contact, and thereby place the accent on intersubjective relationship, opens up an "other" definition of the psychotherapist, differently organized from the old "expert of the psyche" concept recognized by the majority of the psychological and psychiatric world. To posit a self as something more or less internal, more or less superimposed on the notion of a subject in the way we were describing above in the context of the individualist paradigm, leads the psychotherapist to develop objectifiable "knowledge," or at least what she or he considers to be objectifiable, as do other psychotherapists.

Thus his/her intervention will be that of an expert, based on knowledge of an object called "the human being." From the perspective of the postmodern paradigm, the accent will be laid on the dialogic co-construction of experience, as I have been describing all through this presentation. Here it is no longer a matter of expertise, the psychotherapist as architect of change — the definition which is at the center of the debate about psychotherapy today. This in turn will permit us to base the constitution of our profession along the lines of our own distinct and autonomous nature, which derives from our own position and activity in the field. There too, Lewin can help us elaborate our own professional self-concept with his idea of "action research," which has no subject matter independent of its own activity.

e) A necessary vigilance with regard to the question of meaning

I have often referred, in the course of this discussion, to the question of meaning. It was long customary to contrast the notions "discovery" and "construction." The question of meaning moves us inevitably to the domain of hermeneutics, or the study of interpretation, which has meaning as its subject. Our present Conference of the European Association for Gestalt Therapy took as its theme "Hermeneutics and Clinical." This reference to the term hermeneutic leaves me somewhat uneasy, in a way which is not easy to specify. Paul Ricoeur (1965) has shown us the ways in which the hermeneutic domain itself is fragmented today, with the result that various hermeneutic approaches can take us in quite different directions. But again, I believe that placing this question at the center of our therapeutic concerns may result in the introduction of a subtle fragmentation of process. In effect, given that hermeneutics derives from the "science" of the interpretation of written texts, which then becomes extended in the various directions of the vast question of the "meaning of meaning," a certain connotation always clings that has to do with its origins in interpreting the written word. I am very fond of the definition of human nature proposed by the Belgian philosopher Henri Van Lier, "the signed animal" and the idea of reading the human being as an animal covered with signs is not without interest. But the question remains of whether to consider psychotherapy as a decoding or as a construction. I believe — and this is an article of faith — that Gestalt therapy is constructed above all on the concept of experience. And in this sense, meaning itself is only one of the constituents of experience.

To be sure, whatever the value of the appeal to hermeneutics, to postmodernism, to object relations theory, to the psychoanalytic concept of the unconscious, to transference or other concepts, to phenomenology, or to Gestalt psychology itself (which I will not take up here) — we cannot escape (as many writers do) the need for epistemological coherence. We cannot pass from one discipline to another, from one system of thought and reference to another, with complete impunity. The risk we run if we do so is a sort of serial blindness, born out of our fascination with each new set of concepts and terms.

Experience

Lived experience (in German, *Erlebnis,* that which is lived), which refers to the subjective aspect of an event, such as it is actually apprehended in its personal, individual, and concrete significance by the subject, seems to me to be in fact the only organizing concept of subjectivity and of differentiation in the field.

Here I would cite the following lines from Erwin Strauss, the well-known phenomenological psychiatrist, who developed in 1952 a magnificent "introduction to a theory of expression," based on the phenomenon of sighing: "Unfortunately," Strauss wrote, "immediate experiencing is ineffable; it does not know itself, not because it is unconscious, but because it is unreflective. Like Sleeping Beauty, who had to wait for her Prince to break the spell, immediate experience has to wait for the one gifted with the power of the word, to bring it out into the light. The moment this is accomplished, however, immediate experience is threatened by another danger" (p. 10). And from there he elaborates on the impact of tradition, training, interpretation, stereotypes and prejudices which come into play in the expression of experience in words — and thus the necessity of not confusing experience with the awareness of it one has, or with the meaning one gives to it.

Strauss goes on (p. 18): "Experiencing is synonymous with experiencing the world, and with experiencing-oneself-in-the-world. It is directed to the Other; but one experiences the Other only in relation to oneself, and vice versa. This relation, is not a compound of two parts, I and the world, but exists only as a whole."

Lewin (op. cit.) put forth that human events "depend not on the presence or absence of a single factor or a certain number of factors considered in isolation, but on the constellation (structures and forces) of the specific field, taken as a whole."

Out of this dialectic of contact in and of the field, of expression in and of the field, of language in and of the field, through the dynamic complex of confirmations and inclusions, of resonances and empathy, I find myself led by the field to define psychotherapy in the following way: psychotherapy is the experience of becoming apparent to oneself, out of the encounter with another person.

Conclusion

I have undertaken to discuss here how subscribing to a modernist frame of thought can be different from subscribing to the postmodern, along with certain consequences of this difference in the domain of Gestalt therapy. The philosopher J.

F. Lyotard (1979), who was among the first to write on these themes, has carefully examined this concept, postmodernism. He remarks that to say "postmodern" implies a reference to the "modern." "Post" really only means a sequel to something that went before, which implies not a break but continuity, and suggests that the new movement was enfolded in the interior of the old. For Gestalt therapists, familiar as we are with the notion of "post-contact," this idea is easy to grasp, since post-contact as an experience is not independent of contact: it is part of contact, a particular modality or temporal stage in the construction of a specific gestalt — specifically, the stage of deconstruction in the service of assimilation. The postmodernity which I have talked about here, with all the hesitations which go with the use of this term, is thus to be viewed as a prolongation and reconstruction, and not as a break. It is in this direction that McLeod (1995) is writing, in the article I referred to above, even if I do not share all of his conclusions. This is then precisely what is contained in Perls and Goodman's book, if often in a confused fashion: they attempted to combine and dialecticize, in their self theory, particular theoretical modes which derive from Modernism, together with others which belong to the philosophy of Postmodernism. Only through the ongoing dialectic of temporality can we now approach this conception. But to do so, we ourselves need time — and many conversations!

The reflections put forward here are intended as an invitation to a shared process, and not as dogma, of whatever kind. In the final analysis, the invitation of Postmodernism is above all an appeal for deconstruction. The scepticism toward reality which it represents is extended to knowledge, power, self, language — terms which remain for the most part unexamined, and which serve to legitimize and perpetuate our western culture. Individuals construct realities, and these realities are maintained by social interaction — which I in turn confirm beliefs which are themselves social in their origins. Modernism offered us reassurance in our need for certainties, and enabled us to reduce the unknown to what we already knew. Is it possible to leave that certainty, and still move to the encounter with the unknown? Anxiety! Let us remember the title of the psychiatric tale of Hannah Green, which Perls was fond of citing: "*I Never Promised You a Rose Garden.*"

2

"IS ANYBODY THERE?"*

Since the beginning of the 1960s I have endeavored to introduce the concept of expression into the field of the Human Sciences in general and the Clinical Sciences in particular. My trajectory touched those of Guy Lafargue and Jean Broustra at the beginning of the1970s, then, later, those of Max Pagès and others. This endeavor placed me squarely within a certain philosophical and epistemological position whose premises seem clearer now, several decades later.

Here I should like to analyze it from just one of many possible angles. The moment of 1968 seems to me to mark the acme of what we commonly refer to as "modernity." modernity, beginning with the Enlightenment, was a way of

* This article was first presented as a conference paper to an audience of art and performance therapists at the Art Cru Annual Conference 1999.

opening up new perspectives in scientific and technical progress, in knowledge which broke with the largely obscurantist traditions of previous centuries. At the social level, although thinkers, sociologists and social critics may have differing analyses, all would agree on the link between "modernity" and a new emphasis on the primacy of the individual, and the individualism which was one of its unintended consequences.

It is modernity which is associated with the development of reason and science, with the Rights of Man and the associated principles of liberty and fraternity, with the destruction of the social fabric of tribal communities in favor of the concept of society, and hence with the primacy of individualism and the concept of the subject which is so central to modern social sciences. Modernity made romanticism possible, and with it the privileging of emotion and the superceding of the religious by the aesthetic impulse.

Everything was now in place: from this rich soil emerged the interest in expression, creativity, and creative spontaneity, all closely linked to the very definition of the subject.

1. Expression, Exteriorization or Construction

In 1979 I used these words by Michel Tournier to introduce the special edition of *Thérapie Psychomotrice* devoted to the work of IRAE,[*] the predecessor of ADEAC — Art Cru,[**] and despite everything I am still struck by them:

> "What does it mean, to exist? It means to be outside, *sistere ex*, in Latin. What is outside exists. What is inside does not exist [...] What does not exist insists. Insists on existing. All of this little world hammers at the door of the big, real world. And the other has the key."

What seemed crucial to me at that time, even though some writings, by myself and others, were more nuanced in this respect, was the attempt to make manifest, to bring out, to express, as one might speak of squeezing an orange, pressing out the juice which is of course already there (Tournier would say "insistent") inside it. This belongs to the same current of

---

[*] The Institut de Recherche Animation Expression/IRAE (roughly, Institute of Expressive Performance Research: translator's note) was set up at the beginning of the 1970s by myself and Dr. Jean Broustra and Guy Lafargue, among others, and was the first group in France to specialize in research and training from this perspective.

[**] ADEAC- Art Cru (Raw Art) took over from the IRAE at the beginning of the 1980s. It has two strands: a training center for expressive drama therapists, and the museum which puts on exhibitions of the work of "Art Cru."

thought which places at the heart of the subject the unconscious (in a more or less reified form), the primacy of historic-
ity, the notion of (more or less biological) drives, other infer-
ences, other unknowns, potentialities, and hidden traumas.
Exteriorizing, expelling and working through these in a conscious way is seen as both the means and the aim of any "cure."
This is the logic of "uncovering" or "discovering" which Freud
elaborated in a series of archeological metaphors.

However, in a later article, "*Constructions in Psychoanaly
sis*" *(1937), it seems to me that Freud glimpses the direction of
much future thought in emphasizing the idea of "construction"
— and developing it in the course of the article (at least in the
French translation I do not have access to the German original)
— in the sense of "reconstruction." He writes, "His task is to
make out what has been forgotten from the traces which it has
left behind or, more correctly, to *construct* it." [pp. 258-259]

In this article he elaborates the metaphor of the archeologist, and this reminded me of my visit to the Museum of the
Palace of Knossos in Crete, famous for its labyrinth, where a
wall displays a fresco reconstructed by an archeologist on the
basis of a few scattered fragments. A little further on, another
very different fresco is presented as another reconstruction by a
different archeologist using the same fragments, and then, a

---

* "Konstruktionen in der Analyse," *Internationale Zeitschrift für
Psychoanalyse*, 23 (4) 459-469. GW, XVI.

few meters further on, is another version . . . " . . . if the analysis is carried out correctly, we produce in him an assured conviction of the truth of the construction which achieves the same therapeutic result as a recaptured memory" (pp.265-266) as Freud wrote in the article I referred to above.

Nevertheless, we can see here the outline of what was later to take more concrete form, specifically under the influence of the constructivist movement, present also at the heart of the analytic movement, and the opposition between discovery and construction. However, although we can detect its forerunners in various signs and actions, particularly in the areas of art and intellectual thought, it was not until the early 1960s that postmodernity was defined, and with it the loss of illusions — of progress, of science, of truth, mastery and of the dominant culture.

Along with postmodernity came "the desire to re-enchant the world," to adapt Weber's apt phrase. The forms this takes are sometimes chaotic, but the very notion of chaos and its associated doubts and tensions are an integral part of the postmodern paradigm. Many disciplines have seen a process of de-something-or-other: deconstruction, decomposition, decentralization, deregulation, desacralization . . . and disinformation?

I referred above to the constructivism which is one of the active currents of this postmodernity. With it came the acknowledgment that there is no reality other than the one we ourselves construct, sweeping away the myth of the objectivity of sciences and all those approaches which flirt with the scientific method, within the Human Sciences in particular.

In the case of social constructivism, a tendency developed out of constructivism by Berger and Luckmann (1966) and elaborated by Gergen (1992) and others, this emphasis becomes: there is no reality other than the one we create *in relation with others.*

It is this "in relation with others," which makes all the difference, that I would like to develop here.

2. From modernity to Postmodernity

Under the influence of philosophers like Wittgenstein, Ricœur, Lyotard, Gadamer, to name only some of the most influential, the emphasis is on language. "The limits of my language mean the limits of my world," as Wittgenstein put it,[*] meaning that the limits of the forms of our narratives, the statements we make to ourselves and others, our capacity to put into words, define our ability to understand and to explain, and shape the contours of what we call "reality." To put it another way, the words we use, and the stories we tell in order to explain our experience are what can open and close our experience.

---

[*] Wittgenstein 1922, 5, 6.

From this starting point, the postmodern wave engulfs everything articulated around notions of identity and self. In traditional thought, whether romantic or modern, the self is seen as the constant, the deepest part of our being. The "normal" and the "pathological" are both defined in terms of subjects' ability to get in touch with their deepest identity, and the avowed aim of therapy — particularly so-called "modern" therapies — is to enable the subject to achieve this.

From a postmodern perspective, the emphasis is on the changing context, the need to place things in perspective replaces the fascination with personal history, and the "how" of change takes precedence over the "why" of the meanings unearthed. Henceforth we are the product of the contexts of our conversations and the social meanings we derive from them. And as our conversations are constantly changing, our "selves" are in constant flux, are perhaps as changeable as the situations.

As Epstein (1995) remarks, the shift away from describing the self as an object toward describing it as the product of ever-changing social interaction necessitated a radical change within psychology, and hence within psychotherapy. The problem is no longer whether one is or is not in contact with who one really is, with one's deepest identity, but one of regaining flexibility through the fictions, narratives, stories and myths that we use every day to speak who we are.

From this perspective, we lose the assurance of "having" riches deep within ourselves, accessible or merely latent, and thereby we lose our fundamental reliance on the notion of the unconscious. We lose the fictions of identity, and, by the same token, the possibility of gaining objectifiable and measurable knowledge of others. We lose the notion of the norm, and the need to know a "truth" which is now seen as no more than a fiction. We lose the concern with measurement, diagnosis and other practices concerned more or less directly with norms of one kind or another. We lose interest in historical and decon-textualized interpretations. Within the clinical therapeutic situation, we lose the position of power and domination held by the person who knows or is assumed to know, and thus our patients lose the shame of not knowing and of being acted on unawares by hidden forces or unacknowledged truths.

Each of us needs to decide whether these losses should be mourned or if they are cause for rejoicing!

So what does this postmodern perspective offer us in exchange?

We gain the conviction that any theory is a fiction, among other fictions, but it is thanks to and through this theory that we can construct meaning from our experience. As the emphasis is on the co-construction of meaning within the relation, once again we attribute fundamental importance to conversational situations, and thereby to the relationship, to the link, to solidarity and to community, in opposition to what the individualist paradigm offers in terms of autonomy and personal responsibility. What we gain is interdependence. We are focused on the how of experiences rather than the why, on creative invention adapted to the emerging situation much more than on causal explanation. "Here-and-now and henceforth" and no longer "here-and-now because yesterday . . ." Thus therapy becomes the joint creation of a context and no longer refers to an imposed framework. (It is interesting to note that where French-speaking clinicians speak of the "*ca dre*," the "framework," clinicians in the English-speaking world talk of the "setting," with connotations of "placing" and "positioning." Here again, words are imbued with our fictions!)

What is sought is the flexibility of the self, most often seen as a process, much more than some "true self" which needs to be grasped and hence fixed. Psychotherapy becomes more than a linguistic enterprise, it is now a new experience based on two particular experiences expressed in specific words, where the incompatibility of these fictions and representations, as well as the coming together of horizons, enables new meanings to be constructed. The therapist is thus invited to be present not as an expert but as somebody curious and naive, who is exposed to the other's subjectivity in the process of dialogue.

Here again, each reader has to decide whether this conception is a possible advance, or a loss.

3. Postmodernity and the Gestalt Theory of the Self

In 1951 the publication of *Gestalt Therapy* marked the creation of Gestalt therapy and the delineation of its theoretical foundations, putting forward a theory of the self and a therapeutic model based on an analysis of the process of form construction (this is roughly what the concept of "Gestalt therapy" means).

At that time the concept of self was little used within the clinical Human Sciences; its popularity came only later with the work of Winnicott, Kohut and others.

Now, with fifty years of hindsight informed by the theoretical and clinical work undertaken since, this way of conceptualizing the self reveals clearly its dual legacy: its rootedness in a certain individualistic tradition, espoused by Freud among others, and a particular structural approach, both characteristic of modernity, but also its visionary nature and the kind of intuitions which prefigure the current of thought we nowadays refer to as postmodern. Sometimes the juxtaposition of these two tendencies produces a certain dissonance which needs to be refined and made more coherent, but the overall direction is clear.

What is this direction, this epistemological break? In today's terminology, we could sum it up by saying that the self is delocalized, decentred. The self is no longer considered to be an entity, characterized by a certain stability, depth, and permanence: it is a process, constituted "in the field," and no longer conterminous with the concept of the subject, with the power to create forms and meanings, and to create and organize contacts with the human and nonhuman world.

"[The self] is only a small factor in the total organism/environment interaction, but it plays the crucial role of finding and making the meanings that we grow by" (Perls,

Hefferline, and Goodman, 1, §11). Using terms which owe more to Binswanger than to Freud, psychotherapy becomes more of an "analysis of the flow of presence," than an analysis of the psyche, and the "flow of presence," the "being-there," is made up of this continuous experience that we call "contact," which for us is another way of designating the construction of *gestalts*.

To return to Tournier's words that I quoted above, "What does it mean, to exist? It means to be outside, *sistere ex*, in Latin. What is outside exists. What is inside does not exist […] That which does not exist in-sists. Insists on existing . . ."

In contrast to accustomed ways of thinking which "localize" the psyche — albeit metaphorically (the use of the notion of "topic" is another example of this) — the theoretical system of Gestalt therapy prioritizes process and temporality, and includes the time dimension (once more linking *topos* and *chronos*, place and time).

The principal although not exclusive metaphor in Gestalt therapy is therefore temporal rather than spatial, a chronicle or narration rather than a topic. It narrates the organizing of meaning, the field of consciousness, the contacts, and the building of contacts through relationships and interpersonal links . . . Because the self cannot be "localized" within experience: during action or contact it is not experienced in the same way as it is during integration, assimilation, withdrawal, rest, meditation or preparation.

I have often had occasion, and I am not alone in this, to invoke the analogy of methods in quantum physics. When physics addresses light, for example, it recognizes that it can be seen either as a phenomenon made up of particles (photons), or as one made up of waves, a process or movement. When physicists approach it in one of these two ways, they know that this is only one part of the phenomenon, and that they are not equipped to grasp it as both matter and wave simultaneously. Asking which approach is right is to ask the wrong question, and attempting to reconcile the two approaches would lead nowhere. What have they actually "discovered" that makes sense of this duality? Something very simple, but with important consequences for anyone attempting to take a scientific approach: when we speak of waves or photons, we are merely referring to certain instruments that scientists have created in order to study light! Light "is" neither photons or waves, it exists, and it is revealed through the instruments which are designed to measure either photons or waves! This means — and this is something that we in the Human Sciences have known for a long time, particularly since Kurt Lewin, but have an irritating propensity to forget — that in any phenomenon the observer, the witness, however "neutral," is an integral or even a constitutive part.

Like you today, perhaps, at the time I paid little attention to a small "detail" in the quotation from Tournier. I shall repeat it in its entirety:

It means to be outside, *sistere ex*, in Latin. What is outside exists. What is inside does not exist [...] That which does not exist in-sists. Insists on existing. All of this little world hammers at the door of the big, real world. And the other has the key.

And the other has the key!
Without someone else, nothing gets opened. Without someone else, nothing exists. Without someone else, the self does not exist; expression does not exist; speech does not exist.

4. The Other, Co-creator of my Expression

The expressive act as well as the speech act, in my view, point forcefully to the idea that "there is somebody there" opposite me, someone who allows and creates, co-creates, the expression, someone else in whose absence this expression or these words would not be what they seem. In stating this, I am not reintroducing the old distinction made by the linguist De Saussure between language and speech, or between discourse and speech, the former being social and general, the latter individual or particular. This distinction has been too overused to serve my purposes. I would say more precisely that the expressive act, and hence its production, is an act constituted within the field, and that this act involves both a sender and a receiver, to use the vocabulary of communication theory. It is the self, or as one might call it, the self of the situation, on the analogy of Gestalt therapy's use of the term "the id of the situation," not just the id of an identified subject.

I was very impressed by a presentation by two Swiss researchers, Marie-Madeleine and Robert Christe, at a conference in Cerisy* in 1989, organized by P. Fedida and Jacques Schotte and attended by Henri Maldiney, Roland Kuhn, Tellenbach, Blankenburg, Kimura Bin and many other clinicians and phenomenologists. The researchers carried out a study of Rorschach tests in which they compared notes taken during the session with the transcript of the audiovisual recording. To summarize part of their findings very briefly, they were able to show experimentally that in the case of around 70% of responses to the diagrams it was almost impossible to establish whether the replies "belonged" to the clinician or the patient, or even which reply came from whom, or, at the very least, who had elicited the words of whom.

I will draw another analogy. Dreams and creativity have been linked many times. I should like to come back to what Henri Maldiney wrote about Binswanger and dreams, which is similar to one of the approaches to dreaming we find within

---

* The cultural center of the Château de Cerisy in Normandy organizes thematic conferences (literature, human sciences, natural sciences, philosophy etc) and publishes the papers presented. Papers from the conference I refer to here were edited by Pierre Fédida and Jaques Schotte under the title *Psychiatrie et Existence* (see bibliography).

Gestalt therapy. Maldiney reminds us that it was Politzer who first pointed out that the material on which Freudian interpretation is based is not the images of the dream itself but the dream *as recounted by the dreamer*, something that all therapists and analysts know, of course, but which they sometimes "forget." That is to say, the account is linked to the dream, of course, but also to the listener to whom it is told. The account is an interface, in today's parlance. The Gestalt therapist will readily listen to the account as speech directed to the therapist, a telling which cannot do other than hide itself in this appearing, and appear in this hidden, in words not only addressed to the therapist but words in which the patient talks about the therapist, and about themself in relation to the therapist.

"Working out the latent meaning is to reveal the manifest meaning," according to Maldiney. But his important contributions need a more extended treatment.

Expression, like speech, comes out of both "the fusion of horizons," to adopt a term used in hermeneutics, the shared or common ground, to use more Gestaltist terminology, but against this ground it is the figure, whether we see it as created or co-created, which makes possible the processes of differentiation and individuation.

This figure, whether expression or speech, is form, and "the form exists the ground," as Maldiney (1985) puts it so beautifully. "The form exists the ground, just as we exist ours, that is, what is within is, at a specific moment, which is not of itself, and which we bring to life by existing" as he wrote recently in his *Outline of a Phenomenology of Art* (1985).

If the ground is shared, if horizons are fused, and if speech emerges from here, this speech will relate to the field and not just to the speaking subject. An observer within such a situation, as in the case of the Christe research referred to earlier, might be unclear as to who the speech came from. Let us accept for the moment, despite possible caveats, that the words come from the field rather than from one or other of those who constitute it. In order to differentiate the elements within the field, that is, the patient and the therapist in the case at hand, I believe we need to invoke the concept of experience.

I believe in fact that even when we accept fully the hypothesis that the speech is initially a function of the field, nobody would dream of denying that however much the ground is 'shared,' each person's experience of it will be different. Lived experience (*Erlebnis*), referring to the subjective aspect of an event as actually grasped by the subject in the form of personal, individual and concrete meaning, seems to me the only organizing concept of subjectivity and differentiation within the field.

Allow me to quote a few lines by Erwin Straus, the well-known psychiatrist and phenomenologist, who wrote a magnificent *Introduction to a Theory of Expression* (1952), taking the phenomenon of the sigh as his starting point. He wrote as follows:

> Like the Sleeping Beauty who must wait for the Prince to break the spell, immediate experience must await the coming of someone with suffi-

cient powers of expression to bring it to light. But as soon as this takes place, experience faces another danger.

He then goes on to describe the part played by tradition, education, interpretation, stereotypes and prejudices in the process of putting experience into words and hence the need not to confuse our experience with the awareness we have of it.

Straus goes on: "Experience is synonymous with 'experience-of-the-world' and of 'experience-of-self-in-the-world'. It is oriented toward the other; but we only experience the other in relation to ourselves, and vice versa. This relationship is not made up of two parties, the I and the World, it only exists as a whole."

Lewin (1952) maintained that human actions "do not depend on the presence or absence of one factor or a certain number of factors taken in isolation but on the whole constellation — structures and forces — of the specific field in its totality."

It is this dialectic of contact of and within the field, of expression of and within the field, through the complex dynamic of confirmations and inclusions, resonances and *Einfüh lung* or empathy, that speech and expression lead me today to define psychotherapy as "being present on the occasion of another."

3

SELF-APPEARING WITHIN THE OPENNESS
OF A SITUATION

We are fortunate enough to have available to us an open theoretical approach that is comprehensive yet rigorous and can form the basis of a diversified practice that respects our differing styles when confronted with the specificities of our patients. Why I see this as exceptionally fortunate is simply because, nearly fifty years after it was written, our founding text can be reread with the benefit of modern philosophy, sociology, psychology and epistemology and still strike us as surprisingly up to date. Of course we can still find contradictions, incoherences and lacks. Of course, armed with insights from decades of reflection on what it is to be human, on psychotherapy, the subject and society, we can still find archaic elements and references to old paradigms now challenged by current thinking.

What our founders gave us in *Gestalt Therapy* were re-commendations, at least in the tradition bequeathed by Isadore From, a member of the founding group who helped to shape its intuitions and original research: the book includes no exam-ples, so each of us can fill these propositions with content from their own experience and understanding. We all remember Perls' predilection for oral aggression, meaning that he encour-aged us to break down, chew over and appropriate every propo-sition, and never to accept anything without making it our own. Each of us remembers too, Goodman's insistence on the idea of creative adjustment, the mutual transformation of the self and the world, even if only the world of ideas, through the creation of meaning. Each one of us also remembers Laura Perls' invitation to "live at the boundary," meaning that we should take "contact" as the starting point for all reflection and practice. With this inheritance, how could we not continue this process of creative 'chewing over' through interaction with our contemporaries, who include patients as well as theoreticians and colleagues?

In my view, the rupture they brought about, with all their occasional hesitations and clumsiness, consisted of fore-grounding the notion of "field," and hence relegating theoriza-tion of the subject to the status of consequence. This operation does not mean setting up a dichotomy between subject and field and seeing them as opposed and irreducible terms, but rather inverting the order of these factors. The field, and the operations that take place within it, which they grouped to-gether under the generic heading of 'contact,' comes first. The result of this ongoing process is the creation of a subject, and if the process is permanent, so too is the subject. What I am addressing here is thus the possible 'permanence of the subject,' or at least what the subject him or her self refers to as such.

"So what is this gap between myself and me?"

To borrow the phrase the Portuguese poet Fernando Pessoa uses in *The Book of Disquiet*, what is this gap between "myself and me?"

The 'self' as defined within Gestalt psychotherapy has a different meaning from that in common usage. The self is not only an entity, and so cannot be reduced to id-entity. Certainly one of the greatest obstacles we face in understanding the theory of the self in *Gestalt Therapy*, and therefore in using it in a clinical situation, is the range of interpretations of the notion of self. We are assailed by the cultural imperative to identify the self with the subject, the person, and hence to reify it and see it as having boundaries. Similarly, it is difficult for us to think of ourselves as not having a boundary between 'me' and 'not-me' . . . So the therapeutic practice which draws on this system of representations contained within our language is directed at this distinct and solipsistic individuality which we have to understand, analyze, develop, repair, and heal.

Our resistance to the idea that we are not wholes, unitary subjects, subjects with an ongoing continuity, leads Gestalt therapists writing in other languages to adopt the English term 'self' rather than the equivalent in French (*soi*) or Spanish (*si mismo*), which is what philosophers call 'ipseity.' *

However, we are willing to accept that a unified and continuous self does admit of movement, as do all living things. It is this movement, or "self"-movement, which distinguishes a living being from a thing. We situate the origin and "center" of this constant transformation, this inherent ability to change, within the organism, wherever we may place this attribute, and we call it the self.

But 'self' in English connotes a return to the origin of the action. It is a reflexive movement through which actors see themselves as specified, delimited and defined. It is an operation . . . an operation which, paradoxically, presupposes a certain integration into the field in order to achieve a continuous differentiation. Montaigne was referring to this when he said, "I describe not the essence but the passage." ** The notion of self therefore refers to the reflexive operation which accomplishes this differentiation between self and world, and consequently the outcome of this process. Does the psychotherapist intervene at the level of the process, or of its — more or less static — outcome?

---

* *Ipseity* = nature or selfhood: a translation of Heidegger's *Selbstheit*. (Translator's note)

** Michel de Montaigne, Essays, Book III Chapter 2 'On Repentence,' translation by John Florio.

This 'outcome' that we call the self also denotes a differentiation from the other. "Being a self means not being made by another or others, or by the course of events. It is not being 'done-to' (Maldiney, 1992). If this self is "not being made (not being done-to)" by an other or others, psychotherapist or not, although we know full well that we are made up of otherness, that we are manifold, full of introjects and identifications . . . then this self becomes the single operator which transcends these operations in which the other is so present.

At this point I will refrain from once again giving extensive quotations from Perls and Goodman to demonstrate how our founding text constantly swings between these two conceptions of the self: one which thinks of itself as an entity versus one which thinks of itself as an operator; one which considers itself an organism endowed with desires and needs versus one which insists on the necessarily permanent creation of meanings; one which defines contact-with-the-world as a process of 'going towards and taking from,' versus one which sees it in terms of creative adjustment and the construction/destruction of gestalts. Here we can see the (not always dialectical) tension between the respective contributions of Perls and Goodman.

However, what is important here is to clarify the kind of self that psychotherapy works on. If we define psychotherapy as:

- an act of intervening in psychic content
- an act of an expert in personality structure

- the action of a changer for the benefit of the changer/future changee
- the reduction of pathology and the suffering it brings, by reference to some extrinsic norm and a definition of what is or is not healthy

. . . then we are clearly relying on a conception of self which sees it as an entity. We can readily see the attraction of all these theories which tell us about the individual's internal organization, its features and structures, its 'object relations' or other so-called 'internal' structures.

But if, on the other hand, we define psychotherapy as an encounter which allows one "to appear," "to appear in the openness of a situation," or, as I like to put it, "appearing to and with another," then the self's reflexivity will be the priority, this movement of the field which, starting from a place "between," encourages a continual process of individuation.

Hence the process of revealing will attempt to "understand the individual by starting with individuation, rather than understanding individuation by starting with the individual" (Simondon, 1964). Hence it is the process of taking form which defines the being: before any individuation, the being is a rich field of possibilities which can only be by becoming, that is, by individuation. This is what the therapist supports, by 'following' the being as it emerges.

The substantialist tradition encourages a persistent misunderstanding of the notion of 'relationship,' seeing it as two preexistent terms which come into relation with each other. If we follow Simondon in reversing this traditional view, the study of individuation sees substance (which may refer here to the individual as a product of the process) as "an extreme case of relationship: the case of inconsistency in the relationship" (Simondon 1964). He suggests that in order to transform our approach to relationships a theory has to see the human being as the sum of all those actions through which it becomes an individual: "the being is what it becomes through relating."

So an individual consists of relationships. And this 'consists' needs to be understood at two levels:

— the individual is nothing other than the relationship(s) and constantly-renewed acts of individuation which create him or her as the common link between various orders of experience
— it is, moreover, relationships which give a being its consistency, its reality.

The individual, then, is both what is active in the relationship and the result of it. Any change to an individual's relationships with others is also a modification of his or her 'inner' features. In any case, any differentiation between 'inner' and 'outer' is only a matter of degree, because what is outside the individual may become inside, and vice versa. And it is of course precisely this movement which enables growth to occur. This is one of Goodman's basic intuitions: one cannot grasp an individual's reality without understanding the importance of his or her relationship with the environment, because the individual taken in isolation is an incomplete reality, and it is only the act of relating which enables contact operations to be converted into structure, and structure to become contact.

The Openness of the Situation

We may have the illusion of being a thing or a being who is separate from the situation. But our lives are 'situation/organism,' and are engaged within the life of the situation. Freedom is not a property of the organism, but should be seen rather as pertaining to the situation. Alienation is not a property of the organism itself, it needs to be seen as pertaining to the situation. Similarly, development should not be seen as a property of the organism but as pertaining to the situation. Because our lives consist of participating in the situation, engaging with the situation (disengagement is itself a form of engagement with the situation, just as solitude is a modality of 'being-with').

The situation is 'prior to' the subject-object distinction. It is a concept which evokes the field, the field which forms the arena for the processes of integration and differentiation.

Since humans are situational beings, they are the meeting-point for a plethora of viewpoints and consistencies — see Simondon's use of 'consistency' — foldings and unfoldings. Hence truth needs to be thought of as a 'perspectival truth' (Benasayag), that is, as truth from a particular point of view. A situation is always the product of what is. Thinking in terms of the situation therefore means searching for the process which produces that situation, rather than for a localization that validates the person in some metaphysical way. As well as being a process of individuation, the process of production also involves integration and differentiation, belonging and engagement with the situation. This is what gives us freedom. If one of the terms of the 'belonging to the situation/individuation' dyad is missing, there is failure to understand the determinants, the 'done-to' that Maldiney refers to, the 'not-being-able-not-to-do-what-I-am-doing' that Blankenburg sees as the root of all psychopathology.

Becoming free means that in the here and now of each situation, I participate through my praxis (action) in the freedom which organizes the situation.

Jean-Paul Sartre, in *Being and Nothingness*, was one of the first to express this: "There is no freedom other than in situation, and there is no situation other than in freedom . . . I am absolutely free and absolutely responsible for my situation. But I am never free except in situation" (Sartre, *Being and Nothingness*, 1959:509).

By drawing on this concept we may define an act as a response, part of a dialogue with the situation. But an act is not determined by the situation alone. This would strip the notion of intentionality of all meaning. So we are drawn back to Goodman's "id of the situation," a somewhat paradoxical notion which partakes of both the corporeity of the id and the contextual. "Situations do not force us to act, but nor are they merely the stage on which we enact our intentions. We perceive a situation only as a function of our current readiness and willingness to act" (Hans Joas). When we act, and reflect on our actions in the light of the demands of the situation, our sense of self may crystallize, confirming the 'self-appearing' which it made possible.

In fact every situation replays the lack of differentiation between myself and the world that theorists have posited in the case of babies, and, at the same time, every situation simultaneously replays the work of differentiation. We can also see here an analogy with the paradigm of romantic love which continuously negotiates a path between a total merging with the other person and an unconditional capacity to see the other as a separate person. We could also draw on Minkowski's valuable concepts of 'disjunction' and 'bond' to theorize these two basic movements within the field.

The Renunciation of Knowledge

In order for the situation to be open, and hence for the field to create forms, it seems to me increasingly that there are certain necessary conditions:

1.   Renunciation of the power of the therapist, the position of superior knowledge and mastery over the other. I believe that power produces arrogance and generates or activates the humiliation of the other. This does not mean banning therapeutic competence, but deciding what this specific competence consists of: does it mean being an expert in psychology, psychopathology and other disciplines that take the individual as subject, or

being an expert in mobilizing creative forces within the current relationship?

2.   Renunciation of the belief that psychotherapy is a science. That does not mean promoting it to the status of 'art,' as some would have it, thereby justifying anything in the name of some kind of generalized subjectivity. If it were a science, it would have an 'object' of study and a body of techniques. 'Techniques' implies that these are 'reproducible' when used by other people, and implies also a standardized body of knowledge of proven efficacy. Psychotherapy is a practice. I am aware that refusing to claim scientific status for psychotherapy is somewhat risky in the current climate, when the powers that be want to clean up the profession and differentiate us from the gurus, healers and other charlatans. How do we explain our specific approach without disqualifying ourselves in the eyes of other professionals? Bion remarked in one of his seminars "What is a course of psychotherapy? It's two people sitting in a room who talk . . . or don't talk. It seems so simple that it's difficult to believe how hard it is!"

3.   Ensuring that the theory or theories we use to think with do not blind us to what is there before our eyes. It seems to me that theories of whatever kind are constructions or metaphors which help us to make sense of our experience, but as soon as they cease to be meta-

phors and become certainties, they may actually prevent us from being open to the situation. Introversion, the unconscious, internal objects, the psyche, the field . . . are only ways of speaking which reflect our ways of thinking, but which also affect our ways of thinking and perceiving.

Self disclosure

If we work at the level of the field, in the here and now of the situation (although this is not always the case, not always necessary and not always desirable) and part of our function consists of clarifying the process of individuation, that is, the differentiation of the field, what are our tools?

One important tool is the therapist's self-disclosure. What do we mean by this? It is the therapist putting into words his or her own awareness of the current situation in terms of the impact of the situation and hence of the interaction, the way in which he or she is contacted, and how both therapist and client are contacted by the situation, so that both parties may work together on how both may become actors. This is the key word: actor! A person who does, someone who takes action . . . in a situation where people all too often feel acted upon, by the situation, by the context of their lives, their histories, the people around them or their traumas, their unconscious or their symptoms.

This self-disclosure on the part of the therapist, which happens whatever their ethics or deliberate choices, is something I choose to set certain limits to:

— it is essentially limited to the here-and-now of the situation
— as far as possible it is expressed in such a way that it does not become a figure within the situation (this would shift the focus away from the patient) but remains a part of the background that may be drawn upon to enrich, contribute to or, indeed, influence the figure which the patient constructs on the occasion of the situation.
— It is filtered through my guiding theory, and through the work I did on myself in the course of my own therapy.

I am aware that this self-disclosure is linked to my own work of differentiation, what we might term my subjectivity, which is undoubtedly emotional. I shall refer here to what Goodman said about the emotions, namely that "emotion is the immediate and integrative awareness of the relationship between organism and environment" and "it is a function of the field." Quoting again, "the emotions are means of cognition. Far from being obstacles to thought, they are unique deliveries of the state of the organism/environment field and have no substitute; they are the way we become aware of the appropriateness of our concerns: the way the world is for us. As cognitions, they are fallible" (Perls, Hefferline, and Goodman XII, §7, p.188).

Given that emotion, and hence the subjectivity revealed by the therapist, is fallible, it seems advisable to adopt a position of uncertainty. Peter Lomas, a major British psychoanalyst, recommends a stance of "committed uncertainty." I shall pursue this line of thought. Uncertainty is not the same as doubt. Uncertainty refers to what is not known in advance, is subject to conjecture and hence is still open, whereas doubt entails a reluctance to get involved, a questioning of the reality of a fact or the truth of a judgement or action. Doubt may eat away at lived experience whereas uncertainty opens it up. In this respect, adopting the felicitous term used by Frank Staemmler, a German Gestalt therapist, uncertainty needs to be cultivated, with all the different meanings expressed by the word 'cultivated,' including fostered and cultured.

Commitment — Being-for — Solicitation

I shall therefore describe this uncertainty as 'engaged.' We know that Gestalt therapy considers "being engaged within the situation" as one of the three fundamental attributes of the self: it is spontaneous, middle in mode (Perls, Hefferline, and Goodman, X, 4)* and passive, and engaged within the situation. So what does this engagement, this involvement, consist of?

For me psychotherapy is defined, among other ways, by the fact that there is a person who cares about another, and

---

* See Perls, Hefferline and Goodman, (X, 4).

who thus takes on a certain responsibility for the other, and is there for the other. When I refer to the psychotherapist's responsibility, I am not saying that the therapist decides for the patient or organises them and acts as a substitute for the very ego-function we want them to recover. It does not necessarily mean that I have to know if I will be able to do something for the patient, or if I am going to do it or not. Levinas (1990) makes a valid distinction between "being responsible" and "taking responsibility for." All I am saying is that it is incumbent upon us as therapists to set up the situation, to define and provide a context for the relationship, and establish that this situation is for the patient's benefit. And the fact that the therapist receives remuneration for this work guarantees that this is all that is expected from the patient in return. I do not ask my patient to consider me and treat me as I do them, as I might expect in an ordinary I-You relationship. What phenomenologists call "being-with," a term often adopted by Gestalt therapists, is preceded by a "being-for-the-other" on the part of the psychotherapist, one of the modalities of the true "being-with" which is the goal. The modality of "being-with" another, which forms part of responsibility, is what Levinas terms Ethics, meaning perhaps that there is no single ethics of psychotherapy, but that psychotherapy itself is a form of ethics, because it is one manifestation of "being-for" another.

Certainly, "being-with" is one stage beyond "being-for." But being-with, being at someone's side, in a situation of perfect symmetry, is a rare occurrence in human existence: in psychotherapy we are face-to-face, and this is not just a spatial analogy. The psychotherapist solicits, calls forth. In the rather different context of the hermeneutics of Talmudic texts, Levinas uses this beautiful concept of solicitation to describe "the attempt to bring [the text] to life by means of correspondences and echos." The therapist solicits. The term, derived from Latin, means: to move, agitate strongly, perplex, torment, draw to the attention.* In the Middle Ages it was even used to mean "take care" (of): "solliciter un malade" meant to take care of a sick person.**

The Atmosphere

Since the therapist has specific responsibility for setting up the situation, we need to discuss what this involves. I have never been convinced that a situation can be defined essentially in terms of frameworks and rules, even if these concepts do

---

* As can be seen in this passage, the verb 'solliciter' has a different range of meanings to the verb 'solicit' in English, which has rather negative connotations of unwanted attentions. 'Solliciter' is usually translated into English as 'seek' or 'approach.' However, I have translated it here as 'solicit' since this is the word used in English translations and discussions of the work of Levinas and those influenced by him. Levinas himself describes 'soliciting' the text for its meaning as an active process of blowing or rubbing. See Emmanuel Levinas, (1990) *Nine Talmudic Readings*, Indiana University Press, Bloomington, Indiana. [Translator's note]

** This meaning is retained in the English words "solicitous" and "solicitude." [Translator's note]

play an important role. This is probably not the place to open up a debate on these concepts and the ethics they imply. Boundaries need to be established in any situation, the question is how to do this.

I should like to focus here on the concept of 'atmosphere,' introduced over thirty years ago by the great psychiatrist and phenomenologist Hubertus Tellenbach. In his work, "atmospherics" refers metaphorically to the climate, the ambiance and the environment of the interpersonal situation. This can be either submitted to or created. The atmosphere is made up of multiple elements which are difficult to put into words and itemize. The atmosphere is something shared by both parties to the situation, it surrounds them and at the same time it exists between them, and hence contributes to the meanings they create, the quality of the contact and the complexities of the situation.

Of course, I have no intention of reducing the situation or the question of framework to the single issue of atmosphere. I merely wish to continue emphasizing or naming certain forces within the field. Making rules explicit also contributes to creating an atmosphere. What atmosphere? What is our complicity with this process of social reproduction? How do we want to define the situation? What are the openings we want to offer, and which of the inevitable foreclosures do we choose?

Creative Adjustment

Creative adjustment is at the heart of Gestalt theory on the means and goals of a cure, and refers to the capacity, also known as the "self," to simultaneously be transformed by and to transform the environment. In our small world, under the pseudo-cultural influence of the New Age banner, creativity is often seen as a badge of individuality and self-affirmation, the expression of a unique individual self which comes to regard doing macramé or pottery as essential to self-development, growth and self-realization. However, I turn here deliberately to one of the founders of the humanistic psychology to which many Gestalt therapists owe allegiance, Abraham Maslow. He made a distinction between three types of creativity: primary, secondary and integrated.

Primary creativity refers to the deployment of primal imaginative processes, the faculty of representation, playfulness and enthusiasm.

Secondary creativity refers to the rational production of new realities in the world, solving technical, scientific or artistic problems, or even the simple difficulties of daily life.

Integrated creativity, according to Maslow, "needs not only the flash, the inspiration, the peak experience, it also needs hard work, long training, unrelenting criticism, perfectionist standards. In other words, succeeding upon the spontaneous is the deliberate; succeeding upon total acceptance comes criticism; succeeding upon intuition comes rigorous thought; succeeding upon daring comes caution; succeeding upon fantasy and imagination comes reality testing" (Maslow 1998: 158).

It is this form of creativity that I expect from Gestalt therapists like ourselves, a creativity that is associated with and part of adjustment, rather than an insatiable search for new kinds of experience. Such creativity is willing to give up certain options or to adopt a limiting coherence, yet maintains the tension between creativity and conformity since it is aware that this tension cannot be suppressed except by denial.

Self-Appearing within the Openness of the Situation

Self-appearing within the openness of the situation is therefore an operation which is simultaneously active and receptive, a middle mode operation, as Perls and Goodman would say. Often *situation* and *event* are counterposed: here, in the psychotherapeutic situation, we could say that the situation becomes an event and that event gradually becomes advent. "In the act of sensory reception there is both the becoming of the subject and the happening of the world. I only become to the extent that something happens, and nothing happens to me except in my becoming" (Erwin Straus).

But above all, the real only exists for the person who meets it in the course of becoming. "The real is what we did not expect," wrote Maldiney (1973) But it is so tempting to think of the real as what we expected! And psychotherapy may be an opportunity to look before it becomes "a way to language" (Heidegger): "the look as it is put into words" as the poet Francis Ponge put it.

Other human beings as persons cannot *be* revealed. They reveal themselves, or not. They

become open through the rending of their opac-
ity and become themselves in the light of this
rending. But they only disclose their true counte-
nance in the gaze of others. In the gaze, not
beneath the gaze. (Maldiney 1991)

I will close this chapter with the words of Maldiney,
words in which he described his concept of "transpassibility" *
which might make sense to psychotherapists:

"We are open to the unexpected. Transpassibility refers
to this infinite capacity for openness of someone who is there,
'waiting, waiting for nothing'" (Maldiney, 1991:419).

---

* Maldiney's concept of "transpassibilité" is here translated simply as "transpassibility": the meaning lies somewhere between "receptiveness,"
"permeability," and "openness." (translator's note)

4

FROM FIELD TO SITUATION

For many years, particularly under the influence of Freud, psychoanalysis and the psychotherapies which followed from it had been built according to a so-called scientific model, in which the observer considered himself as outside, not involved in the field of experience.

In this perspective, the therapeutic relationship is readily reduced to transference issues, transference issues are reduced to a re-enactment of intrapsychic conflicts, intrapsychic conflicts are reduced to childhood history etc. These successive reductions, if they allow the therapist to build up a lot of hypotheses about the human psyche, do not allow anything like the immediacy of the therapeutic meeting.

In my opinion, psychotherapy is confronted with an alternative and has to choose:

— Either it leans on a one-person-psychological model, such as the Freudian one (even if what I refer to as the Freudian model is often a misunderstanding of Freud's works) which limits the therapist to a certain type of presence and function,

— Or it is in line with a two-persons psychology model as opened up by Ferenczi, and pursued by Balint, Winnicott and many others, and in such a model the therapist will no longer be outside the field of experience.

Our founders offered us a work which fluctuates, swings between these two poles. Perls' influence and definition of contact as a "going to . . . and taking from . . ." incline more toward an "object seeking" theory, such as Fairbairn's, which is not very much a great epistemological shift from the Freudian drive theory. Goodman's influence, on the other hand, describes through his view of contact as a creative adjustment, the creation of meaning out of experience in an organism/ environment field.

Where they both converge is in the emphasis on the field and its immediate consequence: a specific theory of the self. But due to their specific premises and prejudices, Perls' field and self will often slip into reification, while Goodman's field or self will be much more considered as in an ongoing flux.

Which Field?

That's why still today, Gestalt therapists have such different ways of considering the field and consequently the self.

For some of us, reference to the field will only be the recognition that their patient has an environment, a culture, a history, a set of acquaintances and relationships which require be taken into account, and figures which are made in the ongoing process have to do with this environmental background; the concepts of background, environment and field become quickly synonymous. For me, I rather choose to call this perspective: "context." [*]

For some others, reference to Kurt Lewin is more obvious. But, inasmuch as I have a correct understanding of Lewin's works, the Lewinian approach is far from being homogenous. Field is considered as a "field of forces" which are exerted on a given subject. The reference to the magnetic/physical field is an interesting metaphor when used in a one-person psychology, but becomes more perilous when in a two-person one. The field, when it becomes of a group or of a two-person system, escapes with difficulty from becoming a substance or a thing! In addition to this, if — as Lewin recommends — we

---

[*] In order to complete a differentiating among concepts, I'd readily adopt the one offered by Barwise (Barwise J., *The situation in Logic*, Stanford CSLI publications,1989, pp. 149-150):

— Context is made from what ensures to make meanings from "articulated constituent" of information carried by a situation.

— Background (or ground) is made from elements used to articulate the "unarticulated constituents" of this information.

— Circumstances ensure to determine the "articulated no- constituents" of this information.

include the observer in the field, a field such as perceived by observer A and as perceived by observer B are differently and subjectively appreciated. So when one speaks of such "a field" (A's field or B's field), it no more comes close to the use of this concept when speaking of a group or interpersonal field.

A third approach, if I reduce into three rough families the use of this concept of field, has a meaning closer to the phenomenological one. This approach speaks of the field of consciousness or of experience. In this perspective, which could also be labeled as "subjective" or "experiential," field would be this "lived space" of perceptions and actions, of feelings and meanings of any given individual. According to this definition, what "field" is for any given individual can hardly be experienced by another, and can only be approximately approached through empathy, understanding, comprehension, intuition, inference or any other modality generally used to approach the subjectivity of another's experience.

When they speak about contact and some other field phenomena, Perls and Goodman on several occasions introduce the distinction between "in the field" and "of the field." To speak of "subject," "organism," "contact" as events "of" the field and not "in" the field makes it clearer, that the former will keep it as a flux, while the latter leads into a reification.

To try and have a better understanding of some phenomena in a field perspective, I can use tools and constructs from these different approaches, even from others which I did not mention here as the theory of morphogenic fields, since they are about one of our main interest: how fields can create forms, give shape to our experience, etc. But let's go further in our research for consistency.

The Therapeutic Situation

How do we speak about this so-called field which is made of one patient and one therapist? We have to notice that, even though Perls and Goodman put the issue of field at the very center of the theory they were building, they rarely mention it directly. On the other hand, when one look carefully to their text, one discovers that they very often use the concept of "situation," with which I will stay for a while because, in my view, it opens up a great possibility for clarification and refinement of our perspective.

The therapeutic setting, whatever else it is, is first of all a certain kind of situation. Being aware of how this situation impacts us is also a way of understanding how we could have been impacted by some situations in the past. Being aware of how we create or co-create the situation in the here and now is also a way of restoring or enhancing our abilities for creative adjustment.

I was very puzzled when I really paid attention to a little phrase from Perls and Goodman when they speak about the Id: "The id of the situation," without any further details! (Again, it is the id of the situation, not the id in a situation!) It's up to us to solve or understand this amazing proposal which transports us far from the path cleared by Groddeck or Freud, far from the drive theory and these so-called inner forces which lead us.

I then discovered that many times they use this concept of situation. For example, one of the characteristics of the self is to be "engaged with the situation;" neurosis is described as a "situation of chronic low-grade emergency"; psychotherapy itself, most of the time is primarily described in terms of situation, such as in these few lines which one can find in their introduction of the book. (Perls, Hefferline, and Goodman, *emphasis mine*)

> *The therapeutic situation is more than just a statistical event of a doctor plus a patient. It is a meeting of a doctor and a patient. [. . .] Neither a full understanding of the organismic functions nor the best knowledge about the environment (society etc.) covers the total situation. Only the interplay of organism and environment constitutes the psychological situation, not the organism and environment taken separately.*
>
> *In order to do this, we change our outlook toward the therapeutic situation [. . .] That way the clinical becomes an experimental situation.*

I often have been surprised to notice that most Gestalt therapists, while willing to improve their skills, tend to learn more about "the organismic functions" (biology, studies about brain or other functions, theories of psyche, etc.) and seldom look for a better *knowledge about the environment (society etc.)* through sociology, ecology, anthropology etc. Every one of these approaches is of great interest, of course, but our founders drive us, through these words, not to stop with what they will call later on "abstractions" (including organism and environment as well) but to go and explore more about "the situation."

This concept of the situation is so commonplace that it seldom attracts attention. It is a kind of given ground, implicit and rarely made the figure. However, for some dozens of years, several researchers, particularly from the Chicago School of Erving Goffman, have put this concept of the situation in the very center of their work. It is indisputable however that interest in this approach is found in John Dewey's work. And we must also keep in mind that Dewey was of great importance for Paul Goodman's intellectual background. So, for instance, this distinction drawn between "in the field" and "of the field" seems to come directly from Dewey who underlined that an organism does not live in an environment but *by means* of an environment.

Engaged with the Situation

When Perls and Goodman, delineating the characteristics of the self, describe it as "engaged in the situation," they specify: "we mean that there is no sense of oneself or of other things other than one's experience of the situation" (Perls, Hefferline, and Goodman, 10,4). I am made by the situation and take part with the other in the creation of the situation as well. Even before any construction of a gestalt within a therapy session, a situation has already started to be built and will be ground for the forthcoming figures. Self will unfold — or not — in connection with the situation, whatever it is. If we agree with a conception of self as an ever-changing function of the field, a function called-up when and because some creative adjustment is at work, we will be particularly careful in developing propitious conditions for actualizing or restoring the self. Neurosis, defined as a loss of self-functioning which allows routines, secondary physiology, patterns of habits to provide minimal adjustments, can be seen as a denial of the situation. The neurotic acts as if there is any novelty in the here and now situation, as if this situation could be reduced to some of its constituents, fixed once and for all as patterns of thoughts, feelings and actions.

Let's come back to the definition of neurosis as a "situation of chronic low grade emergency" and to the consequences for therapy drawn by Perls and Goodman. In a new situation of unbalance, danger, threat, survival that our authors call "emergency," any organism creates a whole and adjusted answer: whole, since it put into play perceptions, proprioceptions, representations and thoughts, motoric activity etc.; adjusted, since the possibility at the contact-boundary which is actualizing this way allows a spontaneous and creative management of the event. Capacities for orientation and manipulation in the field fully unfold and resist any disruption of the field.

But by means of repetitions and failures in restoring some balance or taking refuge in blotting-out or hallucination, some chronicity of the disequilibrium and of the adaptative gestalt will set in with low grade intensity. There will then be a double tension: danger AND frustration, which empower each other to the extent of neurosis. That's what Perls and Goodman call "chronic low grade emergency" and offer as one of their definitions of neurosis. In this situation, any contact-boundary experience tends to simplify the field experience through two emergency functions: deliberate blotting out and undeliberate hyperactivity. "If the neurotic state is the response to a nonexistent chronic low-grade emergency, with medium tonus and dull and fixed alertness instead of either relaxation or galvanic tone and sharp flexible alertness: then the aim is to concentrate on an existing high-grade emergency with which the patient can actually cope and thereby grow" (Perls, Hefferline, and Goodman, 4, 12).

Thus psychotherapy becomes an opposite emergency, which re-enacts many of the parameters from the chronic emergency but which, in this new experimental safe context, will deprive the patient of his obsolete answers in order to promote his creating of new answers, adjusted to the novelty of the situation. We have to ". . . concentrate on the structure of the actual situation as the task of creative adjustment; to try for an altogether new synthesis and make this the chief point of the session" (Perls, Hefferline, and Goodman, 4, 11). This ability, let's insist, is exactly what Gestalt therapy calls "self." This restoring work of the self thus appears much more bound to a deep-rootedness in the situation than to any kind of expertise of someone about another's psyche.

Taking into account the situation, "the id of the situation thus" begins from the very first moments of every therapeutic meeting and is an integral part of what we call "fore-contact." But fore-contact cannot be considered only as a *moment* inside the contact sequence, because it is also a specific modality. Sometimes, even during the further stages of the gestalt development, we have to "come back" to the situation in order to make it more definite, more explicit, thus helping to clarify and intensify the figure/ground. Developmental theorists regularly insist on the idea that any stage does not replace the previous one but is added to, and that contents of every stage go on being worked out, even during further stages (e.g., see Daniel Stern). During an interview, years ago,[*] Erving Polster stated that probably the most important thing he had learned from Paul Goodman was to consider adulthood as something added to childhood, not something afterwards . . . This logic of "in the same time as," as opposed to the "instead of" indeed permeates the whole of *Gestalt Therapy*. Growth, which is built in an ongoing flux according these modalities, is the same process as in a Gestalt construction which is done over a short period of time, i.e., the therapy session. The situation, while being considered as a ground for the therapeutic meeting, is being built all through every session. It's often useful to make the constituents of the situation more and more

---

[*] JM. Robine, 'Un album d'entretiens à propos de Paul Goodman,' *Revue Gestalt* n° 3, SFG, 1992.

explicit as they go on, since the situation creates us and is our creation as well, by the same token.

What Does it Mean to Focus on the Situation?

When a patient sits in front of me and tells me that he is anxious, I can choose to listen to his words not only as words *in* a certain situation, but also as words *of* the situation, *as if* these words were belonging to an undifferentiated field which has to be explored, instead of to an individual, the one who tells them. The individualist classical position would focus, as I used to do during many years, upon the patient's anxiety: how does he feels it, where does it comes from, what does it remind him of, which projections organize it, etc.? From this position, the therapist comes to consider that he gets a more and more definite knowledge of his patient. If it may look like *natural* because it is so *usual*, this position is only a *choice*, based on a prejudice.

Another choice, tied up with another prejudice, is to look at this anxiety as belonging *first* to the situation. Maybe this anxiety is his response to seeing me? Maybe am I making him anxious? Maybe I am making him anxious as a reaction to my seeing him? or to our meeting? Maybe his anxiety is actually mine? Or may it only be the atmosphere which is being created between us?

Choosing the situation as a starting point has nothing to do with any kind of truth: it's only a methodological choice, rooted in my theoretical choice. What I generally call *myself* might often be considered as a premature differentiating of the field. "Experience is prior to the 'organism' and the 'environment,' which are abstractions from experience." (P. Goodman, 1972).* Ongoing and progressive differentiation, back and forth from integration to individuation, resulting in the destabilization of any fixed set of self-representations (This is me / this is not me), are the very core of the therapeutic work and of self-construction through reflexivity.

This choice is slightly different from the dialogical one, although a number of the dialogical proposals might meet/connect here. The dialogical perspective, even if it takes into account the issue of field, operates to my eyes as if there were already two clearly defined individuals, identified, two subjects who meet each other and thus transform their experience. This belongs more to an "in the field" epistemology than "of the field." Two individuated people, instead of a progressive individuation of these two people. Temporality is not understood in the same way even if, in a situational perspective which I advocate, a dialogical component is easily implemented. One cannot avoid thinking here of one of these main functions of verbalizing that many theorists used to put in a prominent place: to speak is to fill the gap between self and other, overcoming the original separation, sometimes deluding oneself it could be possible for a moment . . . but this claim is also con-

---

* Goodman P. *Little prayers and finite experience*, Harper & Row, New York, 1972, p.7.

demned to failure, a never-ending attempt, like a Sisyphus who would endlessly roll his speech.

In this individuation process, indeed there are moments in which I am I and you are you, we can meet, but there are also times where I am you and you are I, others where only exists a he, a they, an it, others where a we exists, even illusory, others where I have no idea of who I am or who you are!

These movements *of* the field (or *of* the situation) which enable this reflection toward one and the other as distinctive subjects are movements of contact. I already had many opportunities to insist on the fact that Gestalt therapy is much more a verb culture than a noun one, an acting culture than an entity one. In this logic, when I listen to a patient, including to his tellings of anecdotes or dreams, I readily focus, as a figure, on the verbs which are used as clues for the movements of the situation. If a patient, in his telling me a dream for instance, says that he dropped his pen, far from considering this detail as "insignificant," I could linger on it and explore its rambling developments: an unaware wish to drop his therapy? A feeling to be dropped by me, etc.?

In addition, this focusing upon the situation in order to identify its constituents brought me to being much more sensitive to what is here, in preference to what is not here. Premature attention to what is not here often includes an implicit "should be here," almost inevitably shaming. Noticing that the patient looks insistently at the painting which hangs behind me is not exactly the same as noticing that he does not look at me. Noticing that he adopts a tightened breath is not exactly the same as noticing that he almost does not breathe. Noticing that he speaks uniformly is not exactly the same as underlining that he does not allow his emotions to flow.

More Thoughts about "The Situation"

It will be easy for any Gestalt therapist, who is used to approach every human activity (thinking, acting, speaking, feeling, exploring environment etc.) as a contact-boundary phenomenon, i.e., modalities of contact, to consider these as "situated activities."

In order to get down to work on this idea of situation as a ground for my practice as a therapist, I have been exploring the works of various researchers in Human Sciences (sociology, ethnomethodology, semiotics, philosophy, ecopsychology and so on). Among many books which I have read, mainly in English, I relied most on a French study: *La logique des situations Nouveaux regards sur l'écologie des activitéssociales* edited by Michel de Fornel and Louis Quéré and published by L'Ecole des Hautes Etudes en Sciences Sociales. This book has the great advantage of being an introduction to many works scattered over many books. I have still a number of leads to pursue, as a Gestalt-therapist, which of course needs further development.

A situation is "a portion of environment that agents find themselves and that they specify through individuation patterns, without being able to deduce from them any objective knowledge nor to fully articulate into the propositional of their statements." *

a. *The situation controls experience* (Dewey)**

Situation is able to control experience, not merely to happen. Cultural rules govern the way individuals have to behave according to their presence in a meeting. (Goffman 6, 1988a).***

b. *The situation is a representational object.*

Situations are what subjects adjust to through the definitions they create. This definition (meaning giving) is therefore prior to any act of will (Thomas & Znaniecki).****

c. *To act is managing a situation.*

A human agent does not just analyze the situation in which he is, but actually builds it up. Relevant features, cut out

---

* Summary from several phrases in Barwise J., *The Situation in Logic*, CSLI/Stanford, 1989, pp. xiii-xiv

** Dewey, J. Art as experience, New York, Capricorn Books, 1993 and *Logique, la théorie de l'enquete, Paris*, PUF, 1993 (1938)

*** Goffman E. La situation negligee, in *Les moments et leurs hommes*, Paris, Seuil/Minuit 1988 (1964)

**** Thomas & Znaniecki, quoted in de Fornel M. & Quere L, *op. cit.*

and selected to create a situation, form the immediate context for action.

d. *To understand a situation means being able to explain action.*

K. Popper[*] goes as far as considering that if one analyzes the acting subject enough, one might explain his action out of the situation, without any use of psychology: any action is adequate to a situation. An individual is both in a field of possibilities and in a field of coercions (cf. above: experimental emergencies, from Perls, Hefferline, and Goodman)

e. *Situations are indeterminate*

Ethnomethodology on the other hand considers that situations are highly uncertain; they progressively reveal and discover themselves according to an involvement in some ongoing action. Leaning on Gestalt psychology and phenomenology, ethnomethodologists consider that circumstances, situations, events show a relative transparency due to an immediate connection of feeling and meaning, of perception and movement. Meanings of situations come from the coexistence of all these, from which arise a tacit understanding.

f. *Meaning is a relation between situations*[**]

---

[*] Popper, quoted in de Fornel M. & Quere L

[**] Barwise J. *op. cit.*

g. *Does meaning come under perception or comprehension?*

Wittgenstein,[*] who drew a lot of his inspiration from Köhler's and the Gestalt psychologists' work, engaged in an ongoing debate about an important issue; for him, one may speak of perception of meaning without involving any inference. Perception of a meaning is an intrinsic part of the perception of things, unlike Köhler's assertion according which meaning comes from a specific act of meaning-giving, which would come after a perception of sensory units. Wittgenstein is very close to the phenomenological assumption of "ustensility" which makes us comprehend in a single act a chair and its "for sitting on." We'll see later on how this idea can also be at work in the concept of "affordance." We directly perceive objects, events, situations, along with their intrinsic meaning.

h. *Affordance*

"To afford" is to have means to do something. This concept of affordance, in continuation of Lewin's work about "valence," seems to have been used first by Gibson.[**] Affordance refers to the way the environment can be perceived according to our available possibilities to intervene. For Gibson

---

[*] Wittgenstein, L. (1989) *Remarques sur la philosophic de La psychologie.* I. Mauvezin, Ed. T.E.R. (§869)

[**] Gibson J.J. quoted in Quere L. in de Fornel M. & Quere L., *op. cit.*

however, affordance of things from the environment is directly perceived, and any meaning is outside the perceiver. Active perception of situations is thus controlled through the search for affordances. One is, with Gibson, far from the constructivist argument in which there is no perceived reality out of the one we construct. However critical studies of the use of this concept have highlighted that affordances of objects, events and situations depend on intentions and perspectives, standardized and socially organized.

Conclusion

> Situations do not provoke our acts, nor do they represent a simple background for the fulfilment of our intentions. We perceive a situation only according to our abilities and present aptitudes to act. (H. Joas)

I'd like to come back once again to one of my favorite examples. A woman, in her sixties, during our first or second session, was speaking at great length of her weariness at the numerous intrusions from her children and grandchildren who were invading her life and engulfing her. It was a beautiful late afternoon in summer and a particularly intense ray of sunlight came and hit her face, dazzling her without eliciting any awareness from her. ("Seen but unnoticed" as situation theorists would say). It would have been enough to move her seat only from a few inches to avoid this intrusion from the sun, which provoked awful grimaces from her. But "we perceive a situation only according to our abilities and present aptitudes to act," as Joas said, and obviously, her lack of abilities to act was forbidding her from perceiving the situation . . . It would probably have been of little effectiveness to work directly with her about her family system, her difficulty in establishing limits and boundaries as long as her immediate contact with the situation, as shown in situ, was not more conscious.

A Gestalt therapist works on the figure construction process (Therapy — or analysis — of a Gestalt. Perls, Hefferline, and Goodman I, 7). But it's not so much figure as such which calls for our focus as the relationship between a figure and the ground which constitutes and bears it. An isolated figure has no meaning. The artist Marcel Duchamp, taking the lavatory bowl out of the home lavatory to expose it in a sculpture museum, demonstrated this in a striking way. It's usually this kind of foundation that a Gestalt therapist starts from, which also marks out attention to the specificity of the here, in the here-and-now of every meeting.

5

Some Aspects of the Concept of Regression

Science fiction frequently addresses the question of time, usually as a plot device when authors dispatch their characters several millennia into the past or future. Other than time machines — these are always subject to malfunctions — another stylistic device often used by these authors is to imagine the simultaneous existence of different timelines. Hence, in the same place there would be different temporalities with no contact between them, allowing the hero to pass from one timeline to another occasionally and thus modify the course of history by deploying the knowledge acquired within one timeline within another. How to pass from one timeline to another remains a crucial problem; this is usually solved by means of 'time portals' which are scattered over earth's surface, and the search for them is the pretext for various intrigues. These portals also allow intruders from another age to invade the age in which the story is set, and enable the heroes to encounter all kinds of dangers by jumping into the unknown of another age where they do not belong.

Thus, alongside the linear conception of time that dominates our normal thought processes we can glimpse another, equally a human invention, premised on the coexistence of different temporalities within the same space. These different temporalities do not intercommunicate except in exceptional circumstances.

Fifteen years ago, when I wanted to make Paul Goodman's work in Gestalt therapy better known to French-speaking Gestalt therapists, I retraced his steps and interviewed a number of people who had known him in order to gather their testimonies (Robine, 1992). Among these it was Erving Polster who drew my attention to Goodman's conception of time and thereby profoundly altered my way of thinking, opening it up to perspectives that were different to the one I had unconsciously adopted and which to me seemed self-evident. I quote: "There are several essential things that [Paul Goodman] left me with, that he communicated in a unique way, and one of them was about the role childhood plays in a person's life. As he used to say, being an adult is not replacing childhood, it is childhood plus."

A careful reading of *Gestalt Therapy: Excitement and Growth in the Human Personality* (Perls, Hefferline and Goodman, 1951) will show that this is the logic that operates throughout the book: a logic of 'at-the-same-time' rather than "instead-of." So, briefly, being fifty is not being no longer forty, or thirty, or three, it is being forty, thirty, twenty, ten, five or two at the same time. In this view, behaving like a two-year-old should not be seen as regression, as we are still two years old as well as however old we are today. As in the science fiction books I mentioned above, the time lines are superimposed and operate simultaneously.

Using the term 'regression' is far from neutral in terms of psychotherapeutic thought. What about these words from Perls and Goodman — should we see them as an invitation to regression?

"*The childish feelings are important not as a past that must be undone but as some of the most beautiful powers of adult life that must be recovered.* What is required, as Schachtel has said, is to recover the child's way of experiencing the world; . . ." (Perls, Hefferline and Goodman, 1951:297; authors' italics)

One of the major difficulties that therapists face comes from the unthinking use of concepts derived from clinical practice. Is this a paradox? Clinical knowledge is built up by observing patients. The description and analysis of the data obtained is most often framed by one-on-one psychology, that is, an individualistic perspective. We imagine that our findings are 'objective' and independent of the clinician who collects them. But from a field perspective it is the therapeutic encounter that makes it possible to create a pathology of experience, and of course no psychotherapist can deny that their presence has an effect on the creation of the data. Furthermore, the intentionality of both protagonists cannot be the same in a therapeutic situation as in a psychiatric examination.

What I am convinced of is this: certain concepts, while they may be of relevance within clinical or psychopathological approaches, are not necessarily constructive within a psychotherapeutic setting. They may, in fact, channel the thoughts and perceptions of the therapist in directions which run counter to therapeutic ends. Experiments have clearly shown that, for example in teaching, judgments of the level attained by pupils (the 'diagnosis') structure the expectations of the teacher, and thereby the pupils' success or failure, these results thus confirming the original diagnosis even if this is false. I think therefore that to formulate a 'diagnosis' in terms of 'regression' (or 'polarities,' 'internal objects' etc.) goes against the very principle of therapy.

Simply using the term 'regression' evokes the idea of a return to a previous state, by whatever means. Even though in the course of his writings Freud did not limit his use of the concept to temporal regression and added 'topic regression,' 'formal regression' and, later, 'libidinal regression,' the idea of a career, of development and hence of temporality, lies at the very heart of this notion.

The concept of development itself generates certain representations which lie at the heart of our anthropology, and hence of our theoretical and methodological choices. Implicit in the original theory of Gestalt therapy, as I recalled above, is the idea that development is not only succession but also simultaneity. Being an adult does not follow after being a child. It is being a child plus. The corollary is the fact that, at a given moment, past, present, and project come together to form presence and experience.

In the course of therapeutic encounters, the therapist may find that certain specific episodes may still evoke the idea of regression. What is apparent to the therapist's eyes appears as a repeated insistence, and recalls ways of functioning appropriate to earlier stages of development. The only 'how' that I can actually observe, phenomenologically speaking, is this insistence. 'Regression' is not a directly observable experience. It is an interpretation — my one-sided construction of the meaning of the other's experiences. The kinds of questions I then ask become, within the logic of the field, "If there is this insistence, that is it that I am not hearing at this point? What is the 'that' of the situation that cannot emerge . . . or rather, that I am preventing from emerging?" In this way we can discover the real meaning of the concept of 'repetition,' that is, 'ask again,' 'present another petition.' At moments like this, the subject seems to have lost the ability to adopt certain modes of behavior oriented to creating the Gestalt (others might say: mature modes) and therefore has recourse to those that seem most effective at the time.

Rousillon (1992) suggests that Freud, in his *Meta psychological Supplement to the Theory of Dreams,* put forward an alternative to the regression model. Just as the dreamer retiring to bed takes off the accouterments necessary for confronting the demands of daily life, so therapy offers the possibility of "deconstructing the protective superstructure of accouterments which mask the truth of the relationship to oneself and one's history." And as a Gestalt therapist I would add " . . . and mask the possibilities of contact with the world in general, and with the other in particular."

This idea of taking off, of divesting oneself, immediately reminds me of the idea of catharsis, and in fact those episodes referred to as regressive are frequently linked to a cathartic abreaction. The abreaction performs a kind of clearing away of fixed ideas and sweeps away secondary accouterments, thus opening the way to unfinished situations and fixed *gestalten* and allowing them perhaps to move forward. The cathartic abreaction may therefore be considered as one of those potential 'portals' which gives access to other timelines, to continue my science fiction analogy.

Facilitating abreaction is, moreover, one of the components of the group therapy situation, through the acting out of affect, the mutual support that makes it possible to take risks, the (not always relevant) deconstruction of accouterments, the reduction in transference games and so on, and is one of the components that needs more thought in terms of how it invites regression.

To conclude these variations on a theme, I am happy to endorse Daniel Stern's words on the relationship between clinical work and therapy:

It is important to recall that an assessment of clinical theory from the perspective of direct infant observation says nothing about the value of clinical theories as therapeutic constructs. (Stern, 1985:231)

And again:

The traditional clinical-developmental issues [. . .] have been disengaged from any one specific point or phase of origin in developmental time. These issues are seen here as developmental lines — that is, as issues for life, not phases of life. (Stern, 1985:256)

The value of reflecting on the use of concepts like regression lies in calling into question the epistemological foundations of psychotherapy. It seems to me that it is high time to detach psychotherapy from clinical work and psychopathology, not in order to ignore or criticize them but to differentiate it, to rescue it from the status of "applied psychopathology" and to embed it in its true specificity: the encounter situation as the primary means of development.

6

INTENTIONALITY IN FLESH AND BLOOD: TOWARD A PSYCHOPATHOLOGY OF FORE-CONTACTING*

Working in a field perspective requires a radical change in our approach to the therapeutic encounter. We need to focus on what is called "the situation," and the concept of intentionality should take on great importance. The personality function of self often leads to repetitive intentions through acts or meaning-making that prevent contact with novelty. For this reason, Gestalt therapists could fruitfully 'go back' to the concept of intentionality, as prior to any formation of conscious intent or agency. My assumption is that the intentionality of one who is in the presence of another person has to be sought through affectivity, that is, through the way in which the other is affected by the encounter. Far from any premature differen-

* This chapter original appeared in the *International Gestalt Journal* 2003, 26/2. (Translated from French by Bettina Bergo)

tiation or assignation of responsibility, unaware pre-or non-conscious intentionality should be approached as it becomes more and more aware, and available to new and provisional differentiations. As a result of this proposed shift, some new ground is given to a psychopathology of fore-contact. The therapist's self-revealing receives new meanings.

> And while he gazed at her,
> She conceived a soulchild.
>   (Michaux, 1972, p. 114)

On his deathbed, an old patriarch summoned his three sons and bequeathed to them his worldly goods: seventeen camels. The eldest was to receive half the number, the second son a third, and the youngest son one ninth. Having pronounced these words, he passed away. The children remained quite perplexed. But they managed to find a wise man as intelligent as he was impoverished. He possessed but one camel. The three sons appealed to him for help in resolving the problem — apparently insoluble — of their heritage. The wise man simply added his camel to the seventeen others. From then on the division of goods, according to the final wishes of the deceased, became child's play. The eldest son received half of the eighteen camels, that is, nine. The second son, one third, or six camels. And the youngest received, finally, two animals or one ninth. Yet the figures nine, six, and two make up a total of seventeen, as was foreseen by the patriarch. And thus, the eighteenth camel, that of the wise man, was automatically eliminated. One no longer needed it, however indispensable that camel had once been. (Boss, 1959, p. 79)

This Arabic legend is related by Medard Boss to facilitate our comprehension of the role of the analyst, and to cut short what he called, "All the chatter about the 'transference'" (ibid., p. 79). Without the introduction of another person, the situation is a dead end; without the generosity of that other, without his gift — a thing indispensable that must rapidly become "dispensable" — the impasse remains. Such is the presence of the psychotherapist. Such is the unfolding of the therapeutic encounter.

The clinical and psychopathological analysis of the experience of another person, insofar as it is possible, can only be effected within the *encounter*. On Heidegger's (1987) own account, it was precisely this that Ludwig Binswanger, Boss's longtime comrade, overlooked in his attempt to elaborate a psychotherapy under the sign of phenomenology. In his Zollikon seminars, for over a decade, Heidegger received at his home, several times per year, an audience of medical or psychiatric students. In these seminars, Heidegger decried Binswanger's "total lack of comprehension of his thought" (Dastur, 1992, p. 165; Heidegger, 1987, p. 115, more details p. 228), an incomprehension tied to the fact that Heidegger's *Daseins analytik* (see Heidegger, 1962, pp. 67ff.) had nothing to do with solipsism or subjectivism, but rather with a being, with other beings. "For me, it is a question of you, and for you, of me," he was accustomed to say. Psychotherapy can only be approached as discipline for two persons (see Robine, 2001a), and it should be theorized as such. An impossible wager? A thousand-year-long tradition of speaking of the other as though he existed outside the gaze we cast upon him, which is a gaze formed by the co-created situation, has led us to approach the other as though he could be revealed to 'me' outside of me, outside my intentional aim, and outside our encounter itself.

Goodman proposed a Gestalt therapy that stands opposed to that tradition. At the heart of his work written with Perls (Perls et al., 1951) the paradigm of the organism/environment field postulates the priority of indifferentiation in the experience of the I and the You: "Experience is prior to the 'organism' and the 'environment,' which are abstractions from experience" (Goodman, 1972, p. 7). It is from experience that the work, which takes place in the therapeutic encounter, should begin (it owes itself that departure), and it is from there that I would like to start, to develop this essay.

Part I: Psychotherapy Approached as a Situation

A number of thinkers in the social sciences today agree that we should consider the personality as arising so strictly from the situation in which it is engaged, that it can never wholly depart from it and can thus only ever react to its situation from *within* its situation. In a prior study (Robine, 2001a), I underscored the importance that the founders of Gestalt therapy attributed to the concept of situation, to the point of seeming to prefer the reference to "the situation" over the concept of the "field" in their reflections. Psychotherapy is firstly the construction of a situation, and we can readily apply to the latter the definition of situation given by Debord: "The concrete construction of momentary life environments and their transformation into a higher passional quality" (Debord, 2000, p. 33).

What we call the social situation is a structure of possibilities that I create with the other, and which in turn creates us respectively. Clearly, the therapeutic situation defines my presence and my intention as a psychotherapist, just as it defines the presence and expression of my client. The situation hardly invites the latter to give me his "pot roast recipe," but he may come to do so nonetheless. If the tradition impels us to think of this event as resistance or as some other critical mode of contact, another gaze could just as readily call our attention to our patient's project, to his intention, as well as to our own solicitation.

Nevertheless, although the patient's "I am" — which gets declined according to the personality mode of the self — is one of the results of his experience, it is no less (and fundamentally) a play of representations and rhetorical attitudes. If narrative identity, as it is called today, can designate one of the possible declensions of the self, it cannot embrace them in their totality. Gestalt therapy comes to temporalize and delocalize the approach to this concept of the self, thanks to the radical turn that it imposes on the self (see Robine, 2001b, p. 9). Narrative identity, contrariwise, is readily envisioned as static; it frequently lets itself be apprehended as a structure, or a character, thanks to its fixity, which is at least sufficient to give us the impression of permanence and continuity in time. Rightly or wrongly, I recognize the same 'I' in him who I was a few decades earlier. This is, moreover, why Yontef defined a structure as a "slowly changing process."* This need for stability and continuity forecloses access to the novelty of situations and opens us to the repetition of experiences, including the most painful ones.

The subject approaches situations in which he finds himself in light of his narrative identity; and in the patient-therapist face-to-face, the psychotherapist is likewise readily credited with another narrative identity, generally implicit, tied to the presuppositions and needs of the subject. These presuppositions have more 'reality' to them than does

---

* "Process is often contrasted with structure, but in Gestalt therapy field theory structure is seen as merely slowly changing process with states and structures losing the appearance of process because they are framed in a way that does not show the dynamic aspect of the process. The difference is in how they are framed" (Yontef, 1988, p. 29).

observation, since perceptions or sensations in the situation are rarely called forth as reliable material.

> "I would like to touch on such and such ques-
> tion," says the patient, "but I am afraid . . ."
> "Could you identify how it is that I am causing
> you to feel fear?"
> "Oh, you're not doing anything . . . It is I! I am
> always afraid of speaking of these things . . ."

This condensed version of an interaction, while typical in its banality, is born out of representations the patient has of himself and which bring him a certain comfort. It contains the a priori denial that the other could intervene in any way at the level of the experience that is lived in the moment of the situation. A certain form of 1960s and 70s psychotherapy and of Gestalt therapy in particular advocated this "taking responsibility" for what can be thought, sensed, felt, enacted, or lived. It seems to me to go against the perspective of the field, in that it constitutes what I would call a "premature differentiation," because it rests upon an equally premature individuation.

If the process of differentiation and individuation concerns the psychogenesis of each one of us, and if it is progressively and for the most part elaborated in the first moments of life, it nonetheless seems to me that each situation, each encounter, each experience reopens the metaphoric construction

site, in so far as the subject opens to differences, novelty, uncertainty, or to the unknown.

Intentionality

Developed by Edmund Husserl, who made it the central
concept of his philosophy, the term "intentionality" was introduced into psychology before Husserl by Franz Brentano
(1874/1944) in the second half of the nineteenth century. The
perspective that guided Brentano consisted in separating psychology from the natural sciences. To that end, he sought to
elaborate a psychology that refused to make the psyche into an
object liable to be apprehended by the methods of the natural
sciences and which, on the contrary, would rest on "experience." Brentano was thus one of the first to speak of the exteri-
ority of psychic life, seeking to construct a "psychology without
the soul" that would be a psychology of perception and experience. It is not unreasonable, then, that Gestalt psychology and
phenomenology would each consider Brentano as their precursor. Some hundred thirty years later, it is anything but certain
that Brentano's enterprise succeeded, given the still current,
pseudoscientific propensity to consider the soul of the other
person as some reified object for examination.

"What characterizes every psychic phenomenon," wrote
Brentano, "is what the medieval Scholastics called intentional
presence, and what we could ourselves call . . . a relation to

some content, a direction toward an object . . . or immanent objectivity" (1874/1944, p. 94). Later on, Husserl will refine the concept of intentionality (when he specified that consciousness is not a container, but is rather the signifying intention) by defining it as the tension of consciousness toward that which it signifies: "To have meaning, or to intend some meaning, is the fundamental character of all consciousness," (Husserl, 1950, p. 185) as he summed it up in his famous formula. The present moment contains an inherent future, an orientation, and a direction. We can compare this to Goodman's correction to the famous "here and now": "Here, now, next" (see Stoehr, 1994).

If the developments of the concept of intentionality concerned above all mental-consciousness, and particularly the world of representations, certain authors nevertheless enlarged the field of possibilities. For example, Maurice Merleau-Ponty (1945), in his *Phénoménologie de la Perception* maintains that all signification and every speech act are rooted in bodily intentionality. Lévinas (1965), then Searle (1983), emphasized in turn the domain of sensations. Today, it is clinical psychology's turn to lay claim to intentionality as the object of its own definition (see Chemouni, 2001).

The choice of this concept implies the ground principle according to which the human being could not be reduced to its physical nature ("the organism"); that it is, instead, always in relation to an "object," whether real or imaginary. The human being is always *directed toward* something; for instance, toward

ON THE OCCASION OF AN OTHER

an object that has neither existence nor 'objective' meaning in itself, but acquires these thanks to the intentionality that aims at it. In fact, and clinical practice brings this clearly to light, the existence of an object, represented or representable, is not the essential condition of intentionality. One may sometimes speak of an ". . . intentional state or content without an intentional object" (Chemouni, 2001, p. 46). Often enough, a more or less elaborate labor of unpacking is necessary, in order that an object might find its intentional state.

Intentionality in the Situation

Every situation, more specifically every interpersonal situation, mobilizes intentionality in each of its protagonists. The force mobilizing this intentionality can be designated and theorized in different ways. Freud (1923/1991) spoke of it in terms of the drives and, following Groddeck (1963), elaborated his theory of the id, the first reservoir in the psychic economy. (It is, moreover, important to remember throughout what follows in our reflection, that when Freud attempted to theorize the psychic instances [id, ego, superego] from a dynamic and psychogenic point of view, he set up the ego and the superego as progressive differentiations of the id.) In his time Goodman introduced the concept of the "id of the situation" (Perls et al., 1951, 403), a way of localizing the origin of the drive motion in the situation itself, in preference to any localization in the organism or in the psyche itself. The human being *gives form* to the situation as the situation gives form to the human being. "Situations are that to which subjects adjust via the definitions they give to them" (Thomas & Znaniecki, cited by Fornel & Quéré, 1999, 10) This movement of contact and reciprocal constitution founds the human being as actor and beneficiary, as acting and acted-upon in one and the same process.

If the id takes shape in a situation, then it is in the situation too that intentionality becomes an intention. It is there that the id comes to be felt, to be affect, word, contact, act, behavior, or interaction . . . If Groddeck could argue, "man is lived by the id" (1961, p. 35), it is no less true that, starting from the "id of the situation," or from the "drive id" (if we want to preserve the intra-psychic model), modulation and formation are the act of the self, whose constitutive dimension is the id.

In lived experience, the subject readily localizes what is felt, what are behaviors, etc. as its own belongings. The subject explains or justifies them in the personality mode (the "narrative identity"), and situates himself preferentially in an 'I,' which he claims is free and conscious. This blocks off the regulatory force that the situation exerts over his experience. Could we not claim, instead, that one of the functions of psychotherapy consists in dismantling this often-implicit representation, to reconstruct an individuation better articulated through the consideration of successive contacts and situations? Could we not postulate that, in the field of experience, intentionality constitutes what is proper to the subject — constitutes and defines him — and that we place his intentionality as a response to the situation or as an initiative, since intentionality shall give birth to forms?

How to Know the Intentionality of the Other Person?
The Saying of the Felt Experience.[*]

In Gestalt therapy's non-dualistic perspective, that is, in taking up a position beyond what Perls and Goodman called "false dichotomies" (Perls et al., 1951, pp. 240ff.) like that opposing the body and the mind, nothing can be thought outside the bodily experience. It would thus be incoherent to dissociate, or oppose a 'thought-intentionality' or 'deliberated-intentionality' to a corporeal intentionality, even if this lay outside the field of consciousness. Our approach readily gives privilege of place to the patient's statement of what is present to his immediate consciousness. Beyond this limit, psychotherapy proposes a veritable training in the expansion of the field of

---

[*] In this epigram, almost as curious in French as in English, Robine is playing on the subject and the objective genitives. Thus, the expression can mean: "the fact of stating what we undergo or experience," or "the speech, or self-expression, of the experience itself." Leaving these two genitives in flux is clearly the author's intention, as it bespeaks the experience such as he explained it in the previous paragraph. —Trans.

consciousness into the domains of sensation, emotions and sentiments, gestures and behaviors, thoughts and memories, representations and fantasies, perceptions of the environment etc. In the first phase of the construction of the gestalt, it is a matter of allowing the emergence or development of a clear figure that could thereupon be deployed. This amounts to the "drawing together" of partial experiences in immediate consciousness with those that come up, assemble, conflict with, or dialectize the experience in a specific direction of meaning. Every clinician knows how readily the illumination of the coincidence between a patient's anecdote, a bodily experience associated with it, and the gestures that accompany it, etc., structures an orientation noticeably different from the orientation engaged on the basis of spoken words alone (i.e., intentionality verbalized, thereby having become itself an intention) — words which may have been spoken with no regard for the situation itself.

If intentionality is 'directed toward . . . ,' then its meaning should be sought in the situation as a whole, that is, in the field understood as a "structure of possibilities" (Deleuze cited by Miller, 2001, p. 110) where these possibilities cannot be reduced to the single 'organism,' or even the single psyche, as too many clinicians would seek to limit it.

Intuition

Clinicians frequently evoke intuition to designate the modality that opened access, for them, to the other and thus permitted, after all, them to construct some intervention, sometimes highly relevant. Although some would remind us that this mode of access to the other is not free from attributions of meaning and projection, or even from counter-transferential stakes, intuition nonetheless permits a knowledge or awareness, often unrepresentable and inexpressible, of certain components of the patient's experience.

My hypothesis is that this intuition is formed at the crossroads of perception and resonance. The therapist's self-knowledge, which he owes to his personal therapy and his supervision, allows the practitioner to elucidate certain components of resonance that may be in play in the process. It remains for us to come back to what has been perceived, sometimes without consciousness, treated with extreme rapidity and turned into a synthesis that may appear passive. What, then, are the linguistic and bodily signals; what are the vocal and subvocal, the contextual and atmospheric signals perceived by the clinician and immediately synthesized into a global and implicit signification?

It is necessary, moreover, not to lose sight of the fact that intuitions, like perceptions, are organized equally by the knowledge, the science and experience of the clinician. It would be difficult for me to have the intuition that this person before me was frozen with shame — against which he was struggling, that he may have been maltreated or the victim of abuse, or that his depression was the consequence of a crypt or a ghost — if the theories implied were totally foreign to my own reflective markers.

The Encounter With Another Intentionality

The essential postulate of Gestalt therapy rests upon contact. The human being is fundamentally contact, creative or conservative adjustment within an environment. It is in and through alterity that intentionality exists. The therapeutic encounter is an encounter of intentionalities, each calling to the other and in this way refining it. Through the encounter, intentionalities take the form of intentions.

In a prior study (Robine, 2001a), I invoked the concept of *affordance* to enlarge the spectrum of linguistic possibilities that should permit us to speak in terms of a field and not just according to the solipsistic conception. This neologism was forged by Gibson (1979), father of eco-psychology, from the verb to *afford*, which can be paraphrased as "to have the means to do something." It thus designates a characteristic that refers at once to the 'organism' and to the 'environment,' to the fundamental properties that determine the way in which 'the object' can be used. A chair offers support; its affordance lets me envision sitting down, in connection with my intentions, perceptions, and possibilities.

Affordance is at work in the therapy session, as it is in every situation. The patient perceives the psychotherapist and his affordance; this will mobilize those 'uses' that the patient will be able to make of him, while extinguishing others. My perception of a chair can entail the wish to sit down; if I need to accede to an object out of reach, high up in my library, I shall perceive a certain number of affordances in the situation:

a chair, a chest on which to climb. I could even organize inhabitual affordances; perceiving in telephone books a means to raise myself up, or even the possibility of using someone in the room as short ladder. Contact with my environment reveals me to myself and actualizes certain of my potentialities, at the same time as I bestow on my environment potentialities perhaps unexplored up until then. But these attributions nonetheless take account of the possible affordance of the object: I will not perceive in the pocket calculator on my desk the possibility of accessing a shelf beyond my reach. "Situations do not provoke our actions, but neither do they represent the simple background against which we realize our intentions. We do not perceive a situation in function of our aptitudes or our present dispositions to act" (Joas, 1999, pp. 170f.). In the therapeutic encounter, we are each for the other, consciously and unconsciously, the essential, constitutive element of the situation.

The Other Person Affects Me

It is a matter of common sense and experience to recognize that the other person affects me from the moment I am in his presence. He affects me, that is, he brings me to feel, to imagine, to think, to infer, and to experience bodily and emotionally. Even my neutrality — if such neutrality exists — or my indifference, is not the pure product of my will or my choices. My lived experience is a tie. It is tied to my intentionality, to be sure, but also to the presence of the other and his own focus or intending.

My working hypothesis consists in claiming that consciousness of my lived experience in the here and now of the situation is a privileged instrument of knowledge of the intentionality of the other. I would be tempted to juxtapose this assertion to Perls's and Goodman's remarks about emotion, when they say:

> An emotion is the integrative awareness of a relation between the organism and the environment. . . . As such, it is a function of the field. . . . In the sequence of grounds and figures, the emotions take over the motivational force of the urges and appetites. . . . The emotions are means of cognition. Far from being obstacles to thought, they are unique deliveries of the state of the organism/environment field . . . (Perls et al., 1951, pp. 407ff.)

What I feel in the presence of the other is thus an indicator of what is in the field. It speaks of me, speaks of the other; it speaks of the situation, of the atmosphere, and it speaks of our encounter. I agree completely with Perls and Goodman when they acknowledge that, as cognition, emotions are fallible, but one can correct them — indeed, cultivate and refine them. And above all, one can speak or state them as indicators of what is.

When a woman I am following in group therapy begins speaking a confused language on the verge of incoherence, when her incoherence is accompanied by diverse vegetative manifestations, onomatopoeia and stammering, the more I seek to understand her the less I understand. The sole information to which I can hold fast at that particular moment is what I feel, which gradually takes the form of a desire to take her in my arms as I might do with a child, and at the same time the desire to strike her! Now, when I name these for her, she calms down and begins to speak of the abuse she experienced as a child — an abuse she had never brought up before — in which she already experienced violence and tenderness woven together. It was in that direction of meaning that her intentionality, or that of the situation, thrust her confusedly.

Conscious and Non conscious Intentionality

In the working perspective of Gestalt therapy, it does not seem to me to make sense to rely on some differentiation between what it could mean to raise something — as other approaches do — from consciousness or the unconscious up to the level of intentionality; this is a dissociation that Perls and Goodman ranked among the "false dichotomies." Our approach, centered on the process of consciousness or the becoming-conscious, does not require the postulate of a "site" from which intentions might arise that were possibly contradictory to those already present in consciousness. In this sense, the symptom constitutes something unavoidable in regard to the question of intentional aiming, which must bring together what is conscious and what non-conscious in the experience, in order to be unfolded in view of its becoming explicit. The child who at a given moment fails in school is certainly not conscious that he aims to arouse the attention and supportive presence of his mother, in order to forestall with this the intensification of the mother's depression. Nevertheless, as long as some intentionality is not brought to light — which does not necessarily imply bringing it to consciousness — and other modalities of reaching the same, essential objective are not elaborated, the symptom will resist, in search as it is of acknowledgment.

This is why it seems fundamental to me, when we undertake the work of unfolding or analyzing a symptom, clarify its impact upon the patient's repertoire, how it may be experienced, how it affects the other person, and how it motivates actions in response. These shall figure as givens, essential to venture meaning hypotheses about the intentionality of the symptom.

When *Gestalt* therapy states that the symptom begins by being — at the moment of its constitution — a creative adjustment to the situation or an attempt, however awkward, to resolve the problem encountered, it acknowledges implicitly the intentionality of that symptom. The symptom is a 'trying-to-say' or a 'meaning-to-say' addressed to someone.

Synthesis

Basing my remarks on the works of Brentano, Husserl, and some of their successors (without pledging complete allegiance, nonetheless, to their arguments), I have sought to show

how the concept of intentionality could prove valuable in the domain of psychotherapy. Other *Gestalt* therapist authors, notably Pietro Cavaleri (1992), have placed this concept at the center of their thought. Yet it seems to me impossible to follow Cavaleri in his definition of intentionality, since he assimilates Goodman's "deliberateness" to Husserl's intentionality. That way, intentionality becomes, for Cavaleri, a characteristic of the self in the mode of ego functioning. This conception of intentionality probably corresponds to a contemporary use of the term, as when one gives excuses, for example: "I did not do this intentionally." There, "intentionally" clearly corresponds to "deliberately."

For my part, I would situate intentionality as constitutive of the emergence of the figure, and I would thus see it as tied more to the "id of the situation" and to its ". . . next," in a field perspective. If individuation is to be sought, as I have proposed, on the side of bringing to light the reflections of this intentionality, then I can only approach it in the clinical situation in vagueness and confusion. Only by starting from deliberate intentions and working back to that imprecise intentionality — which speaks as readily of self as of the other and of the situation — can we disengage the self from being part of the play of representations established in advance by the personality function, in order to allow it (the self) to accede to an ego mode solidly tied to the id of the situation. It is therefore to a psychopathology of fore-contact that our reflection will bring us; it is that which will constitute the second section of our essay.

Part II: The Vague and the Confused

It is to Eugene Minkowski (1999) that I owe the above-mentioned two concepts — the vague and the confused. They seem to me particularly appropriate for evoking this phase of the process of construction and destruction of gestalts, which is situated at the moment of emergence and/or the construction of the figure; that is, at the fertile exit from the void that, according to Perls, defines the zero point, the before and the after, of every gestalt.

In the therapeutic process, such as the Gestalt therapist expresses it, each sequence is ordered as a 'dance' of figures and grounds. Over the course of the fore-contact, a figure is constituted and gradually differentiated from the ground. The background of the figure — or simply its ground — nourishes and sustains the figure, and it is only in the relationship between the figure and ground that we encounter meaning. The figure gives meaning to the ground, which, without it, would only be confusion and vague associations, just as the ground gives meaning to the figure that it raises and sustains. This figure-ground relationship is intentionality, meaning direction, and excitation-toward. In the following phase of setting in contact, the intentionality of the figure-ground relationship will gain fullness and precision, clarity and firmness, through the unfolding of contact according to predominantly active and deliberate modes.

Sometimes the patient comes to a session with a firmly constituted theme, problem, demand, or emotion. This formation, this meaning constitution was effectuated in advance and the figure that he thus brings with him is, in a sense, the bud ready to burst open.

Yet this figure is already filled with history and representations, language and presuppositions. "The meaning bank is the individual's memory" (Dorra, 2001, p. 69). It is not that I would claim to be able to arrive at a *tabula rasa*, free of the impact of the personality-function in the formation of the experience to-come. There is nonetheless a certain play we must introduce into what might otherwise be a set of gears, too well oiled. We introduce a measure of uncertainty, even doubt. This is what the Gestalt therapist does (sometimes intuitively), when he refuses to take, as is, the figure (or screen-figure?[*]) that the patient brings to him, but rather unfolds it with him. In so doing, the therapist returns in a sense to the conditions of its elaboration. He returns to the bringing to light of the very materials used in the figure's construction. He combs through and rejoins the elements constituting the ground: thoughts, experiences, sensations, gestures, analogical language, associations, verbal and nonverbal expressions, sentiments and emotions, fragments of signification, etc. Aiming to reach the background of the figure provided, this work often redistributes the excitation and — precisely because it takes the situational present and the presence of another person into account

---

[*] Here "screen-figure" is used in the sense in which psychoanalysis speaks of "screen-memory."

— inflects and recomposes the direction of meaning; it complexifies intentionality by amplifying the confusion.

Minkowski clearly showed how what should remain united or whole sometimes finds itself separated; he called this phenomenon, "disjunction" (1999, pp. 683f.). To its contrary — which Minkowski called the "tie" (1999, pp. 684f.) that binds, albeit abusively at times — he opposed what should remain separated. If he showed clearly how these phenomena are at work in certain pathologies characterized as epilepsy and schizophrenia, Minkowski also specified how, according to more indistinct modes, they operate in the *world of forms*. These figures we find brought to us are filled with ties and disjunctions, tied to history, to narrative identity, to context and to many other factors and it is in this precise place that 'play' and mobility should be introduced. To be sure, new disjunctions and ties will not fail to arise, which will perhaps become the objects of new upheavals. It is in the activation of these processes that a fundamental part of the therapeutic work operates (the foundations). And it is there that the term 'work' takes on its full meaning — a term with which I am quite content when I think that one says of a fine wooden instrument that the wood "works."

We now have reality before us anew, in its primary fullness. Now, in accordance with various demands, we cut slices or sections out of this reality. It is in this way . . . that we come to pose the "object" before us. We do this not by separating it from other objects . . . but by cutting out all that gravitates round it, all that envelopes it primitively and attaches it to the whole. That is, we cut out all that living and moving atmosphere into which it is plunged (that atmosphere in which everything seems to have to be confounded), by finding there simultaneously its original source made up of that breath of poetry that passes through reality and belongs to it by the same right that prose does, made up likewise of that sphere in which words forming images and metaphors experienced (and accessible to each of us) find their place and translate, at almost every instant and in so expressive a way, that side of life. (Minkowski, 1999, p. 694)

Would it not suffice, in Minkowski's magnificent description, to speak of the "figure" instead the object, to rediscover, at work, that process of construction on which the patient and the therapist collaborate?

But this disjunction dialectizes with the tie that binds:

Life is in no way made up of objects situated in space, nor of facts situated in time. Life is made of that dynamism that governs everything. In man, we also find the need to follow this path; to attach, to establish a tie. (ibid., p. 696)

Minkowski sketched the conjuncture between confusion and the mechanism of the tie. "In confusion, things that ought to come apart impinge upon each other, they enter into each other and, in a word, get confused" (ibid., p. 699). Experiences get agglomerated, amalgamated, mixed together. No figure can then emerge with precise contours, limits, relief, brilliance or fullness. The Gestalt therapist recognizes there one of the clinical forms of confluence which, according to our founders' terminology, prevents the discovery-and-invention of a figure in regard to a ground. As we showed in a previous study (Robine & Lapeyronnie, 1997), if confluence allows us to bind experience, then it also knows how to alienate experience by holding it in a murky feeling from which the figure struggles to extract itself.

Another characteristic of the confluent experience can be approached through Minkowski's concept of "the vague." Here again,

> the contours, limits, and boundaries prove to be compromised; partly erased, they grow frayed, lack precision, and cease to be clear cut. But this deficiency does not come from the various objects being substituted for each other and getting into a muddle, the dimming or effacement points toward the object itself. (ibid., p. 700)

A word is vague; needs are vague; intentionality is vague and, as long as it remains vague, the figure will have difficulty emerging as such in the subject's field of experience. Yet the figure is there, nascent as it were, since it is in formation. Confusion, or 'the confused,' is no doubt prior since it contaminates the emergence of the figure. From this imprecise emergence, a form with more differentiated contours detaches itself; at first it is vague, but it can perhaps become more precise, that is, unified. The confused is clearly found more at the level of felt, or lived, experience, whereas the vague already begins to limit, extract, to think and to come together into a figure.

The vague and the confused make wandering, straying, and distraction possible. The progressive differentiation to which they may give rise, with the support of the therapist as the figure takes shape, constitutes the essential part of the moment of fore-contact in the construction of the gestalt. Out of the initial confusion, the beginnings of consciousness are extracted. Combing through them allows us to gather up vague forms or experience-extracts that, once assembled, will constitute themselves into a more and more precise and pregnant figure.

The confused and the vague can evoke anxiety, which can lead the subject to make hasty differentiations whose product can itself be immobilized in a fixed form. The form gets fixed, here, because it has served its purpose containing anxiety in a given situation, but now gets repeated, ignoring the transformations in the original situation.

The emergence of a precise figure can likewise generate anxiety. Confluence allows us to interrupt the process by a return to confusion, vagueness, or the undifferentiated.

In the construction of the gestalt, this is a moment both particularly delicate and potentially fertile in the therapeutic encounter, since it sets the process of individuation back to work from
the ground up. The paradigm of thinking — since Aristotle no
doubt — has reduced individuation to the individuated entity.
It is the constituted individual who structures the real, not the
real that presides over individuation. Stability, on which the
notion of the individual rests, is thus considered the very form
of existence. But in every domain, the most stable state is
death. Life, on the contrary, is mobility and process. Each
moment offers the renewed possibility of taking up genesis, of
engaging becoming on the basis of the complex situations in
the present, and thus the possibility of being engaged in a
recomposition of processes starting from states.

The therapist can contribute to this process of disjoin-
ing; he can contribute to the differentiation of composites and
to the separation of linkages. Obviously, it is not a question of
substituting new, presumably more fitting, ties for old connec-
tions supposed to be dysfunctional. It is much more a matter of
introducing mobility in such a way that nascent experience can
modulate its available and accessible materials into creative
configurations, themselves unceasingly renewed.

It is to a truly aesthetic function that the therapist is
invited in this phase of therapeutic experience: he follows the
shaping, the *Gestaltung*, to the same degree that the patient sets
his own aesthetic functions in motion to constitute a figure
from the elements in presence. In his own time, Freud opposed
the painter's act to that of the sculptor. The first works by

adding matter in successive strata, and so, works by additions and layers. The sculptor, Freud explained, proceeds by successive removals: He causes a form to arise by removing matter, shard by shard, shaving by shaving. In the twentieth century, artistic creation diversified the modes by which it created forms: The painter can tear his canvas, glue and cement, scratch and cut. The sculptor can assemble heterogeneous materials (cf. the work of Boltanski, Annette Messager, etc.); he can work by compression or expansion (César, etc.), by accumulations and juxtapositions (Arman, etc.), wrappings and coverings (Christo); he can solder (Giacometti), work with the ready-made (Duchamp), assemble constructions (Panamarenko's war or flying machines, the igloos of Mario Mertz), etc.

And why not extend the metaphor to other formal practices: making the strings of a cello vibrate, dancing, setting the stage, orchestrating, modulating the voice, poetizing, dramatizing, clowning, recounting, producing images, and other metaphors. Each aesthetic practice contains its talents and its limits. Each one teaches us new characteristics of the process of taking-shape. In the same way, the fabrication of symptoms and dysfunction arises from this same dynamic of taking-shape, as Rank (1989) demonstrated and as other Gestalt theorists like Michael Vincent Miller (2001) have attempted to show in their approach to psychopathological phenomena.

This mode of formation or assembly allows us to approach what Merleau-Ponty called "the speaking word" (1945, p. 229). What he is designating with this expression is the word, animated by a signifying intention in its incipience; the word which attempts to "put into words a certain silence" (Merleau-Ponty, 1964, p. 166) that preceded the intention itself. Merleau-Ponty opposes the speaking word to the "spoken word," which rests upon sedimented meanings and ". . . enjoys the available meanings the way one enjoys an acquired fortune" (1945, p. 229). On the basis of these acquired and available meanings, the creator, like the child, is able to produce other expressive acts and to repeatedly transform the spoken word into word that speaks anew. It is useful, in this regard, to read Goodman's pages on chatter and poetry, in Chapter VII of *Gestalt Therapy* (Perls et al., 1951, pp. 320ff.).

Part III: The Intention Nascent, in the Body[*]

Out of that initial chaos — vague and confused — out of that present or recovered confluence, or again, out of that pre-differentiation which we rediscover by working our way back behind premature differentiations, the dynamic of individuation rests upon the formation of intentions, their identification and acknowledgment. If we accept a hypothesis of the

---

[*] In French "en corps" (bodily, corporeally) is homonymous with "encore" (again, once again). The intention is, in fact, born afresh in the *Gestaltung* described in the previous section. The focus, now, is on the relation between intentionality and the body. — Trans.

field and thus of situated activity or the situated word, then a vague intentionality — which, originally, is only a direction of meaning — will be more readily discovered and/or invented on the side of the speaking word than on that of the spoken word. At least we will be searching for the speaking word within the spoken word.

The body "... is not just one expressive space among all the others, but the very origin of all the others, the very movement of expression." "... a primordial, signifying operation in which what is expressed does not exist apart from the expression itself" (Merleau-Ponty, 1945, pp. 171, 193). Meaning animates my body as it animates my nascent word. Intentionality and corporeity mutually awaken each other. It is not with clear meanings or an elaborate thought that the other person communicates with me, or I primarily with him; rather, it is through a certain bodily style of being, with a speaking word whether it be verbal or nonverbal. And my reception of the other person's intentionality is not a reflected thought. It is not a reflective and explicit consciousness, but a certain form of my existence in the mode of "being-affected."

The communication or comprehension of gestures is achieved thanks to the reciprocity between my intentions and the gestures of the other person, between my gestures and the intentions legible in the other's behavior. Everything happens as though the other's intention inhabited my body, or as though my intentions inhabited his. The gesture that I witness sketches the outline of an intentional object in a kind of dotted line. This object becomes actual, and it is fully understood when my body's powers adjust to it and cover it. The gesture is before me like a question, it indicates to me certain perceptible points in the world, it invites me to join it there . . .

as Merleau-Ponty (1945, pp. 215f.) writes magnificently.

It is not so much words or representations that establish primary communication, as a signifying intention that sets words and bodies in motion within an implicit register. There is someone facing the patient and, in an act (conscious or not), there is an intentionality that focuses on and affects him. It is in this respect that the tentative setting into words of the way in which the other person affects me, reflects a certain number of indices that may allow us to shed light on his implicit aim and thereby contribute to its differentiation.

The expressiveness of the body should be distinguished from the intention to signify. To signify, in effect, consists in using a sign to designate an object and its meaning to another person. But expressing does not imply the mediation of a sign. The smile is not a sign referring to some meaning; the smile is the corporeal modality of meaning. It is intentionality lived by the subject, and it will become meaning in being perceived by the other person, and in the return he gives it.

The corporeal lived experience of a subject is rarely independent of the intentionality it contains. In this regard, I would invite the doubting reader to try a very simple experiment. In focusing your consciousness subtly, gently touch, before your eyes, the tip of your left index finger with your right index finger. Keep in mind the distinct sensations you noted in each of your index fingers. Then do the opposite movement. That is, touch your right index finger, this time, with your left index finger. You will doubtless note that, at the contact point, the sensations are different according as your finger is animated by a "touching" intentionality or by a "being touched" intentionality. From a strictly mechanical point of view, the sensations ought to be the same. However, when the touched reverses into the touching, that which organizes the difference arises from a specific intentionality, and not from some objective factor.

But the sole access I can have to the other's intentionality is tied to his expressiveness.

> *A priori, the other person* is defined in each
> system by his expressive value, that is, by his
> implicit and enveloping value . . . The other
> cannot be separated from the expressiveness that
> constitutes him . . . To grasp the other as he is,
> we were justified in calling for specific conditions
> of experience; that is, the moment in which the
> expressed does not yet exist (for us) outside of

that which expressed it. (Deleuze, 1968, pp. 334f. — *original italics*).

Deleuze even adds, "we must understand that the other person is not a structure among others within the field of perception. *He is the structure that conditions the field in its totality,* as well as the functioning of that totality" (1969, p. 58 — *original italics*).

Phenomenology has taught us that it is impossible to separate things from their manner of appearing to someone. This hypothesis sets us radically apart from the belief in the neutrality of the therapist. It invites us, on the contrary, to consider the modes according to which things appear to him as constituting the phenomena themselves. Far from deploring the presence of my subjectivity (including the influence it has in determining the organization of the field), I lay claim to my "being-affected," as a tool by which to comprehend the other. Georges Braque said that the painter did not seek to "reconstitute an anecdotal fact, but rather to constitute a pictorial fact" (1994, p. 30). By analogy, I would readily say that the therapist does not seek to reconstitute an anecdotal fact, but rather to constitute a therapeutic fact.

We are thus distancing ourselves from an approach that would call itself scientific, in order to enter fully into an aesthetic procedure. If I want to comprehend (and I mean to *comprehend*, not to explicate) and feel light, to whom shall I turn more readily? To the physicists who speak to me of photons and undulatory phenomena, or to the works of painters of past centuries? The therapeutic situation is where a taking-form or taking-shape occurs; it is a situation of construction and deconstruction of forms (*Gestalten*), in and through the encounter, which may be conflictual, of two intentionalities.

Provisional Conclusion

A number of philosophical, sociological, psychological or psychotherapeutic approaches have placed the notion of the subject at the heart of their theories and practices. Our thought patterns are constructed on this prejudice. According to these approaches, the self (or the subject, etc., whatever the name we choose to give it) is assigned a forced residence because it has been confused with the individual. It is therefore shut up and alienated. Gestalt therapy, born in the 1940s and 50s, undertook a theorization for psychotherapy that vanished into the cracks that this system of thought had begun to manifest. The cracks became breaks or gaps, and then faults, and finally a paradigm change. Everything should be rebuilt in the perspective of the field: therapy is to be rethought as a situation, practice, as an encounter, expression, as an effect of the field. Indeed, we must rethink expression as an effect of the field before being the manifestation of a psyche — which the psyche generates rather than following from that psyche.

In the therapeutic encounter, the one and the other may be tempted to position themselves as *a priori* constituted, as individuated. This is a modality that has stood its tests over the decades. Another modality can come into being on the bases established by our founders, and their definition of the self. As a catalyst of functions requisite for contact with novelty and for realizing creative adjustments, the self is engaged in the situation. The Gestalt therapist is engaged in the situation, and this engagement is part of the very structuring of the field. He affects the other person and the other affects him. The implicit intention of each party can be stammeringly expressed on the basis of each one's experience, such as he feels and perceives it. In this respect, the moment of fore-contact, the moment of emergence and/or construction of the figure, is determinative. In effect, it allows us to orient ourselves in the 'same,' that is, in what is known, in the narrative. It may also allow us to start from an undifferentiated site, which will have to be individuated continuously, on-goingly. Thus, recalling Medard Boss's tale with which we began this essay, the therapist will have to add his 'camel' to the givens of the situation, and without even knowing what will come of it. His intentionality will simply be to open conditions of possibility — the forms of which remain to be created.

7

"I Am Me and My Circumstance"*

Jean Marie Robine Interviewed by Richard Wallstein

WALLSTEIN: It seems a good place to begin by understanding how you developed as a Gestalt therapist. What I know about you is that you are a clinical psychologist, so I imagine you started off somewhere different than Gestalt and came to it later. How did that happen?

ROBINE: When I was a psychology student, I was interested in three specific areas which were not present at all in the psychological field as such. First was art and what later became

---

* This interview originally appeared in the *British Gestalt Journal*, Vol. 12, #1. 2003

Expressive Therapy. This was not exactly art therapy because at that time I was already much more interested in the expressive *process*, rather than the finished object. So this was art through media like dancing, voice, painting, puppets, and so on. At that time, there was no work in the field which combined this process with the field of psychology and psychotherapy at all. Before, when I was a teenager in the 60s, I already had this kind of practice with groups of teenagers in educational programs; later in the 1970s, friends and I created an institute to try to combine this art/expressive process work with psychology. Some of the experimentation was very crazy, and this period and this work was very exciting and creative. It was the "1968" years!

The second direction I was interested in was body work; during the late 60s and early 70s, there was nothing in the field of psychology in France about body work except relaxation and psychodrama. So I trained in psychodrama; this was, in fact, my first practice as a psychotherapist later on.

The third area was a dimension of group work in both the therapeutic and psycho-sociological domains. By the mid 70s, I had also trained in Lewinian style 'T' groups. In this period, there was a lot of experimentation in group work, and many trainers came to France offering workshops; I tried many of these new approaches, and I immediately connected to Gestalt therapy.

WALLSTEIN: What was it about Gestalt that made the connection with you so immediate?

ROBINE: Mostly, it was intuition. After ten years of group practice with expressive and psychodrama approaches, I was able to help people express themselves, but I had no support or guidelines about what to do with what happened in that expressive work. Nevertheless I had been very reluctant to move into the psychoanalytic pattern which was, and still is dominant in France. All my friends went to psychoanalysis, and, in fact, later, I did have a personal psychoanalysis. But at that time, it seemed too much the establishment way, too closed and rigid.

When I met Gestalt therapy, I had the sensation and insight that *this* was it,' this could be the basis for a practice. Although I had this intuitive feeling, the Gestalt that was practiced then — the Esalen style with its Perlsian demonstration work — did not feel satisfying to me. That work appeared to be about huge emotional catharsis, a lot of body work and exercises. But I had the sense that underneath this kind of practicing there might be a theory that would ground it, and that was what I imagined would be valuable for me. However, at the time, no one was able to tell me, yes, there is a theory.

WALLSTEIN: So it seems like this was a leap of faith on your part.

ROBINE: Yes, I felt there was fresh air in the field when I met this work. So I participated in some workshops here and there in the mid-70s and started practicing in this way, empirically, reading books by Perls and others. I heard at this time of a Belgian organization that had created a training for French speakers. The trainers on the program were French-speakers from the Gestalt Institute of Cleveland. I joined this program for three or four years. It was a tremendous commitment as I had to make the ten hours each way train journey every two months.

Our bible, at that time, was the Polsters' book, *Gestalt Therapy Integrated*, (Polster, E. and Polster, M. 1973) and every workshop, every weekend, we translated a new chapter. The organization of the training program was that of the book; we followed the order of the book.

After I finished in 1979 or 1980, I felt OK but also unsatisfied. I wanted to go further, but I was not at all clear where exactly to go. My dissatisfaction was such that at that time, I even considered becoming a psychoanalyst. My difficulty was that while it seemed fine to work in the way I had seen for an isolated workshop or weekend, it did not seem appropriate for an ongoing, long-term, individual weekly therapy with severely disturbed patients.

WALLSTEIN: What seemed to be missing from the work as you knew it then?

ROBINE: Now I can understand what happened, but at that time I was not clear enough what was missing. The work seemed not deep enough; there were bits of theory and bits of practice, but they were not connected enough. There was, at that time, no attention at all paid to psychopathology; there were no openings to ideas about developmental issues, and so on. What I decided to do was to go directly to the Polsters for one week. But I was not satisfied by this week either; I was disappointed. This surprised me very much, as their book had been the foundation of the structured part of my learning.

I then heard about a guy I had never heard about before. It was a man called Isadore From, and I was told that he represented the viewpoint and the work of Paul Goodman. And I had never heard of Paul Goodman before either! I decided to meet Isadore. We had good contact, and he agreed to my joining a group of his students. We met all over Europe when he was visiting Europe, half of every year.

WALLSTEIN: Was this a therapy group or a training group?

ROBINE: This was mostly a theory and supervision group. Isadore didn't practice therapy in such a context, and he didn't practice what is often called training. In fact, he did not believe it was possible to train psychotherapists. He said there are two kinds of activity for the so-called training of a therapist: teaching and personal therapy. So he was doing teaching, and included in this was supervision. He would do individual therapy if you wanted, but nothing in the group situation, except perhaps for small interventions. I continued with Isadore until he retired in 1983 or 1984. I had several opportunities to go on alone with him, in New York City or in his farm in Dordogne, or in my home, but without our small group. This work and my time with him were really exciting for me. Through Isadore, I discovered the works of Paul Goodman. That introduction was more than twenty years ago, and I am still not finished with this model! In contrast, I felt finished with the Esalen Perlsian model, let's say, after six months and the Cleveland model after one year. Goodman's model, for me, is still open and fresh. Everything is not in their book, of course, (Perls, Hefferline, and Goodman, 1951) and a lot of work is needed to develop this model in new directions, but for me it is still exciting. Every time I go back to the book, I find new elements.

The Self and the Field

WALLSTEIN: What particular elements of Goodman's model stand out for you as particularly exciting?

ROBINE: For me, the way Goodman considers the Self is one that stands out. Goodman says the Self is only a small factor in the field. Though small, it is nevertheless fundamental because the Self is where the process of creating of meanings occurs. I am also excited by Goodman's views of the contact boundary, the self as field process — these are revolutionary. I still find it difficult to understand the Self in this way, rather than as an entity or concept which could be the same as the subject, or the organism, person or soul. We have more than twenty-five-hundred years training in thinking of entities. Sometimes in the works of Perls and Goodman you can read sentences where the Self can be interpreted in this latter way. But sometimes, you have openings for the new direction they introduced. And today, fifty years later, we can look back and see the seeds of what present-day philosophers, or psychoanalysts, are also now trying to develop — within the post-modernist framework, with constructivism, etc. And for me it is very exciting.

If instead we want to consider the Self as an entity or subject, maybe pursuing psychoanalytical models could be more interesting, as they are more developed and there is a great deal of writing. As an intrapsychic model, psychoanalysis is much more sophisticated than the Perls, Hefferline, and Goodman model if you want to read it from the point of view of 'self-as-entity.' I can understand that some Gestalt therapists who use Perls, Hefferline, and Goodman in this individualistic perspective need to complete their theoretical system, for instance by incorporating object relations theory and so on. Personally, I'm not interested in this direction, because most of the work is already done, and well done, regarding the intra-psychic direction or way to thinking about the self; and above all, I am not interested because doing so loses what seems most innovative in Gestalt therapy.

If we are interested in the field and the contact boundary, and the Self as a small function of the field, there is a lot of work to be done, a lot of shifts in our usual ways of thinking. This is something very new and very contemporary, and a lot is unknown about where we go next ...

WALLSTEIN: Could you say a little more about the 'field perspective' and how you see it as innovative?

ROBINE: One difficulty I believe exists among Gestalt therapists, is that we don't all share the same definition of 'field.'

WALLSTEIN: What is your definition?

ROBINE: There are two major kinds of definition and we tend to move back and forth between them. One is analogous to the physical field, and the other is more phenomenological, like the field of experience.

WALLSTEIN: What would be an example of the physical field?

ROBINE: I am tempted to say that the physical field is the context, even knowing that's not the right definition; for instance, here I am in your physical field (i.e., your office etc.), but what happens between us right now is an experiential field, different for you and for me. As a therapist, the permanent question for me hinges around the experience that, when I tell you something or you tell me something, I have the sensation, the feeling, that in the former case it is me as a subject who decides to speak, and while this is my experience, I am not so sure this is what happens. I am interested in seeing how my own speaking and my own thinking is created by the field and not only by myself as a separate entity.

WALLSTEIN: I'm thinking about your article in the *British Gestalt Journal*, "The Unknown Carried into Relationships" and this seems very connected (Robine, 1996).

Yes, there is a lot of mutual *resonance*, and this is a concept I use a lot. I also love Sheldrake's concept of morphic resonance. I think it is very useful. I'm sure if you were another interviewer, I would not be saying the same thing right now, and that if you were interviewing someone else, you would be saying different things. So I am really interested in this process and how it can be used in the therapeutic process.

A Different Kind of Expert

WALLSTEIN: So how could it be used? One of the things I love about your writing is the experience I have reading it, the feeling. So one question I have is how one might use this in therapy?

ROBINE: That is really the big issue and question, how to formalize this thinking. For me the thing that has changed over the past five years is stopping working as an expert. Or it might be better to say, shifting the expertise from the knowledge of how an individual functions to being a kind of expert in what can happen in a relationship. And it is a very different position. I am probably more involved in the relationship. I am using my resonances not to report what I think or feel but using what I feel in a very different way — mostly in order to support the client, so that he can enlarge his experience of the field in the here and now, and also back and forth with the past.

I have always been very sensitive to 'process.' I am reminded of an experiment in a recent training program session. Over three days the students worked with clients, as in a practicum. The clients were allowed, as usual, to say whatever they wanted, and so was the therapist. The one exception was that the client was not allowed to say what their issue was, so nothing was said about their theme or problem. All the therapists had to work with was the process. It was a very powerful experiment — all the therapists could work with was the process in the here and now, without any explicit content.

WALLSTEIN: Earlier in our conversation you mentioned that one of the things you were concerned by in Gestalt was the lack of diagnosis. I imagine that you have built into your program work on diagnosis. From this perspective, would observing the process, as in the experiment you have just described, be enough for a Gestalt therapist?

ROBINE: I have been practicing psychotherapy now for 35 years, so I have a lot in my background. It would be easy to say as Perls did, 'that's bullshit,' or 'we don't need diagnosis.' But it is here and it has been integrated. Diagnosis and psychopathology can give us support in understanding the process in which clients are engaging. It isn't a frame to cure hysteria or other things, but it can give us information. Knowing early processes is also useful. I'm not sure that we need a specific psychopathology for Gestalt therapy or a specific theory of development either. We have several of the landmarks that we need in order to be able to give support to the process. We have a number of concepts to describe the experience of the client, and I can use concepts from psychoanalysis, Binswanger, phenomenology . . . but there is no formalization. There is no vocabulary, for instance, for describing the way the client is able to create a gestalt or a bond, or contact novelty or reduce novelty to things already known. It seems to me that we have a lot of tools, but not an entire descriptive framework. Otto Rank said that every client obliges us to remake psychopathology. Classical diagnostic thinking describes some categories of processes and/or structures, and it's useful to be more sensitive to more processes, to be able to see them. But what we have to engage in is the real work of exploration. Categories and termi-

nology describe different ways of dealing with a lot of fundamental issues — such as bonding, attunement, shame, anxiety,
recognition, and so on — and in therapy we work through
these essential issues. But relying on standard 'symptoms' and
the like is too easy; it is not the demanding kind of exploration
I am talking about.

Phenomenology in France

WALLSTEIN: Are there particular elements of Gestalt therapy as it is practiced in France that distinguish it from
other ways of practicing?

ROBINE: There are several streams of Gestalt therapy in
France; three in particular. One is very close to the California
model of the late 1960s, and this is still very alive in France
with one particular school. Another comes from this first one
but incorporates theories from other approaches such as Jung-
ian or object relations psychoanalysis. Another one is my
school. Probably the particular quality of this school is that we
tried from the very beginning to ground Gestalt therapy in our
cultural context, especially in the direction of phenomenology
and the field perspective. We don't use the word phenomenology in the same way as in America. I don't know how it is used
here in England, but in America it refers simply to the lived
experience, as in 'can you tell me your phenomenology.' In

France, we use it with reference to the philosophical stream of Husserl and Heidegger, Binswanger and Merleau-Ponty. And I have tried to use it to clarify some of the concepts of Gestalt psychotherapy — for instance, 'what is introjection?' 'What is confluence?' The concept of confluence has changed greatly over the years since Perls and Goodman, and the current view is not at all the same as the earlier one. My wife wrote a book about confluence, and I have written a chapter on contact. So you see we are looking at the basic concepts which are used by the community but which need to be clarified. Another instance is 'experience.' What is meant by 'experience?' Phenomenology has a lot to teach us about the meaning of experience.

WALLSTEIN: What does it mean for you at the moment?

ROBINE: Heidegger tells us that phenomenology is a method to unfold experience. For instance what is a phenomenon? Sometimes it is reduced to what is obvious, and it is not always obvious. Sometimes, it requires a lot of work to unfold an experience. In France, we never use the term, 'my phenomenology.' We speak about phenomenology as a method, a philosophy, a position in the world, a way of considering.

WALLSTEIN: And how would you apply that philosophy in a particular instance?

ROBINE: We would try to describe what your experience is, to unfold what is here and what is implicit in it. For instance, the method includes what Husserl call the épochè — putting into brackets judgement, preconceptions, prejudice, and so on. And we might consider our organization in space, our time organization.

WALLSTEIN: So in a session with a client you might explore how they organize their body in space and what their experience of time is . . .

ROBINE: Yes. For instance, when you read a phenomenological psychiatrist or psychotherapist like Binswanger, or Blankenburg or Bin Kimura, they describe the experience of people. For instance, the way they organize time. They describe how a particular type of psychotic can live in the present as if it was a future. They are able to describe such experiences with great precision, using only this kind of reference.

WALLSTEIN: Can you say more about experiencing time?

ROBINE: For me the question of time is critical to understanding the concept of self in Gestalt therapy. It is different from a spatial representation. It is very easy to have a representation in the way Freud had, regarding the organization of the conscious, the preconscious, the unconscious, with each element being deeper and deeper. It is a spatial organization. This structural way of thinking is also evident in psychopathology. It is as if things were stopped, immobilized. If you consider self as a process, you can see that self is not the same in a forecontact stage or contact stage or final contact stage, and the self is not localized at all in the same place.

I remember an interview with Paul Goodman in a book by Glassheim, an American essayist. He asked Goodman, 'If I understand you, you have a conception of the self as de-localized?' Goodman said, 'Yes, the self is not the heart of the person. The self is where the action is.' It means that in spite of our desire to localize the self, we can't, it is shifting in place and intensity as well. When I am deeply involved in answering your questions, where is my self? It is possibly more between us than 'in me.' And when I withdraw and am in a post-contact phase, the self is fading — and perhaps is then more 'inside my skin'? This experience of shifting the self, for me, is a time experience because according to the time, the self can shift its place and change its intensity. When there is no creative adjustment being done, there is no self or very little self. Which doesn't mean there is no subject, no organism, no identity, but just little self. This is my understanding of Paul Goodman's proposals.

WALLSTEIN: Are there any other particular ways that define your practice of Gestalt therapy?

ROBINE: I pay much attention, and spend a lot of time in the fore-contact phase. In my opinion, probably under the influence of the Esalen stage of my training, and of what Yontef called 'boom-boom therapy,' many Gestalt therapists tend to enter too quickly into contacting phases. The more time you spend in the early construction of a gestalt, the stronger, the brighter it will be. The less time you spend at this stage, the more likely you'll work as a behaviourist.

What Distinguishes Gestalt Therapy?

WALLSTEIN: I would like to ask you something else. In thinking about Gestalt therapy, do you consider that the self-as-process idea, so central to Gestalt therapy and to what you have been talking about, is what is most distinctive about our approach? Or is 'working in the present moment' the idea that defines it as different from other psychotherapies? Or are our ideas of the importance of the field what distinguishes us?

ROBINE: For me, our founding text opens a lot of possibilities. Most of us have chosen some specific orientation among these possibilities. Thus, in Perls, Hefferline, and Goodman, as I said earlier, you can easily find that 'self-as-process' coexists with 'self-as-entity.' And we do often theorize as if these two concepts of 'self' were not designating the same idea — in fact, as if there were two kinds of 'self.' What we have to choose is our emphasis at any one time. Of course, we could say that self-as-process is one of the main distinctive characteristics of our approach, but that's not so important if we don't also go on unfolding and unfolding this idea with its many consequences, both theoretical and practical.

Personally, I don't like the term *process* very much, even if I sometimes use it as an easy way out. It's not that very phenomenological. You cannot experience a process; you can only be conscious of it when it's done, or when you look backwards and try to understand what happened. When they write about gestalt-construction or creative adjustment, Perls, Hefferline, and Goodman use the term 'sequence,' which simply means that some event follows a previous one and so on. You can watch the sequence, experience it. And when done, you can then describe the process. I could always say where I am in a sequence, but I cannot say where I am in a process.

I would like to say that what distinguishes us is having the field perspective as methodology and emphasis. But I'm not so sure since I am far from certain that by *field* we are referring to the same construct. Very often, field is nothing but a slogan and the way that some of us in the Gestalt community practice is more in line with a very individualistic model. I would include Perls himself in this category. And I could hardly say that Perls was not practicing Gestalt therapy! Field, in this case, is only taking into account that our patient lives (or lived) in a specific context. And what psychotherapy is not aware of that?

Another perspective is more Lewinian, and due to some ambiguities in Lewin's ideas, field is sometimes reified, as if field were an entity. A third conception about the field is more phenomenological, and I would add is allied with some postmodern influences. In a phenomenological perspective, field is defined by a unique way of structuring experience.

Postmodernity or the Chicago School (Goffman and his followers) would put more emphasis upon the importance of the 'situation' structuring experience. (Did you notice that in Perls, Hefferline, and Goodman, there is much more use of the concept of *situation* than of *field*?) We are created by situations as much as we create them, from moment to moment. So for me the conception of a field is pre-phenomenological.

So, I'd say, 'yes' to field perspective, and 'yes' to 'here and now' — since situation is nothing but the here and now — but with these reservations mentioned above. However, I am not convinced that this can be considered as what makes Gestalt therapy distinctive for all Gestalt therapists. It's a specific feature that I am choosing to endorse radically. There is some field perspective (as a contextual approach) in every kind of therapy, there is here-and-now in every kind of therapy . . . Isadore From used to say that what we call 'here-and-now' is nothing different from what psychoanalysts call 'transference'!

So, a conclusion to my long answer to your question is this. I would say that the most definitive and basic concept of Gestalt therapy theory, and the most revolutionary (at least what has had the greatest impact upon my theory and practice and provoked a revolutionary shift for me) is the concept of the 'id of the situation.'

Differentiation in the Field

WALLSTEIN: The 'id of the situation' appears in Perls, Hefferline, and Goodman, but remains something of a mystery. Can you say more about what it means to you, and how it has been revolutionary for how you practice?

ROBINE: When Perls theorizes about contact-making, or when we see him working, we can understand that his implicit (sometimes explicit) concept of contact has something to do with a 'going to . . . and taking from.' The usual way this is described — with reference to the so-called 'contact cycle' or 'cycle of experience' — starts from the emergence of a drive or appetite or need which is 'localized' inside the subject or organism. It implies that the id function belongs to the organism (even if we accept that, in some cases, it's stimulated by the environment). It suggests that the organism is prior, i.e., prior to the field. This is not very far from Freudian drive theory, with its division into subject/object. A subject going to an object and taking from it. That is a possible way of theorizing.

Then Goodman offers his somehow mysterious 'id of the situation' — 'id' belonging to the situation instead of an 'innermost core.' What a shift, what a relocation! The challenge is the proposal that field (or situation) is prior to the subject. I don't take this as a truth, but as a methodological proposal. It means, as a consequence, that most of the time, what we call 'subject' can be considered as a premature differentiation of the field. Premature differentiation because a so-called 'individual' id of this kind would be in fact much embedded and molded by the personality function (which tends to draw experience toward the well-known sphere of 'Whom I know that I am').

More and more, I try to work from an undifferentiated situation or field, avoiding a premature dividing up into 'this is me' *versus* 'this is not me' (or 'this is you') and working through this differentiating process in the here and now of the situation.

WALLSTEIN: What do you mean that the 'field is prior to the subject'? Some readers will not understand this. Can you give an example that makes it clearer?

From the very opening of their book, Perls, Hefferline, and Goodman set up that 'organism' or 'environment' are 'abstractions' out of the field. In some way, they suggest it is not meaningful to focus on one of these abstractions, instead of contacting. One step further could be to consider *first* the actual present situation (or field). Thus, let's first look as the situation as unique, as not-yet-differentiated into a You and an I, in order to look at the impact of the situation upon the two of us. And, then, progressively, to differentiate the two experiences...

In 1914, the great Spanish philosopher Ortega y Gasset said "I am me and my circumstance." Let's look first my (our) circumstance, since this *circumstance creates myself and him/her self,* as well as *I and the other creating our circumstance.* From a methodological perspective, we used to practice mostly one way: the way we create the situations, (it creates what I call 'premature responsibility'). Rarely do we look the other way: the way situations create us.

With the traditional methodology, the personality-function of the self tends to refer the present experience to what we already know about ourselves. The bank of meanings is the memory of an individual. What I would like to do, as frequently as I can, is to short-circuit the premature intervention of personality-function and to create confusion, 'undifferentiation' or 'pre-differentiation.' For instance, a patient sits and says how anxious he is. A traditional way of practicing might focus directly on 'his' anxiety (events, history, context and the like). Another way might start from a creative uncertainty: how might I be generating his anxiety? How can I be sure that I am not frightening him? Or maybe I am anxious or fearful and I am passing it on to him. It works very well with shame, too!

Of course, this methodological perspective cannot replace the traditional one altogether. But each time we start from the field (or situation) instead of starting from the individual, each time we can consider our own 'single' experience as belonging first to the situation, we can co-construct an ongoing differentiation or individuation. Thereby we get a great opportunity for transformation, a shift in fixed situations and representations.

WALLSTEIN: Thank you very much, Jean-Marie.

PART II

Introduction to the Psychotherapeutic Illustrations

The examples provided in this second part do not claim to be typical. They are not demonstrations of anything. At most, they may show something. We shall see!

Ever since the beginning of the 1970s, when Perls's book of transcriptions of demonstration sessions, *Gestalt Ther apy Verbatim*, was published, the professional world of psychotherapy has been divided as to whether such publications are appropriate.

Some, including myself, were distressed by the havoc indirectly wrought by this book. A large number of readers took these sessions out of context. The 'demonstration' became a model for 'psychotherapy' as such. A meeting which might have lasted five to thirty minutes in all became a methodological prescription for courses of psychotherapy taking place weekly over a period of years. Perls' spontaneous and seemingly hedonistic slogans of those years led readers to ignore his background of forty-five years of practice as a psychotherapist. His provocative and frustrating style, amplified by a readership in search of a happy ending, became a basic technique — a method or even a theory — swallowed whole by several generations of believers. Some American friends and colleagues quite rightly dubbed this kind of practice 'bang bang therapy'!

Others, also including myself, deplored more the lack of published illustrations of Gestalt therapy in practice, which has opened the way to all kinds of fantasies and projections on the part of skeptics and detractors of Gestalt therapy. There are in fact two major difficulties here. The first lies in our theory as well as our practice: we do not separate the subject from his or her surroundings, nor can we separate the patient's expression from the conditions from which it emerges, namely the presence, interventions and questions of the psychotherapist. It is therefore impossible for us to talk about the 'case' of such-and-such a patient as is commonly done, as if the patient were an independent entity, and spoke in a way that did not speak of the psychotherapist as well as of the patient him or herself or of the situation, as we hope the previous chapters have demonstrated. This reification of the patient and his or her artificial isolation from the encounter with the practitioner makes it easier to reach oversimplified interpretations and understandings, even for those within the phenomenological tradition. Here we have a perfect example of what I referred to earlier as 'one-to-one psychology.'

But writing psychotherapy involves writing about the encounter, the atmosphere, the feelings, the resentments, the words chosen or not chosen, the gestures and mimicry, the changes in breathing and the verbal nuances, all the subtleties that make up a domain more familiar to the novelist or the poet than to the psy- something-or-other. So this is the second major difficulty. We do not pay attention to words, content and meaning alone but to as many as possible of the aspects of experience as lived by both parties. But our age-old traditions of naming and writing are unavoidably caught up in an individualistic paradigm, whereas the language of the field has yet to be invented!

The theoretical discussion presented in the first part of the book is deliberately 'involved.' I feel — and I want to be — far removed from the so-called 'benevolent neutrality' often wrongly attributed to Freud, although he himself was often very much involved in his cures. My practice is equally involved and engaged, although much can be said about the forms this involvement takes, some of which may be as harmful as even the most benevolent neutrality.

My involvement extends into these practical illustrations. I have made the choice to present them 'as is,' meaning that I provide no commentaries, explanations or theoretical or methodological justifications, and volunteer no history: I leave it to the reader, professional or nonprofessional alike, to decide whether or not to enter, whether to criticize or enjoy the raw material. However, in the final section, I will set out some of the features of the approach put into practice here.

These encounters are not therapy sessions. This is not to say that they may not have therapeutic effects. They are illustrative moments or demonstrations as found in training seminars for psychotherapists. To me, they are 'ordinary' in that nothing particularly spectacular happens. Any step taken by the 'patient,' if any step is taken, is a tiny one in relation to their overall journey, as may be the case in any one session of a long course of psychotherapy.

So how did I choose these sessions? They were transcribed from video recordings. In fact I have very few video recordings, hardly more than the ones presented here, as I do not find them very useful as a teaching tool. Maybe, in a seminar we might set up the machine just in case we want to go over the material and carry out a detailed analysis, but this would be an exception. Hence I had little choice. I have of course retained the spoken style and refrained from making any corrections to style or content even when, on rereading, I was tempted to improve one of my contributions, out of vanity!

So this is not a case of presenting the reader with carefully selected cases. The aim is rather to use these sketches to demonstrate 'how things work' with a Gestalt psychotherapist and the person he or she is accompanying. Some professionals will surely discern underlying theoretical and 'technical' choices; others will be more sensitive to questions of style, while others still may think that I should have made different choices! I accept these risks unruffled, because for me these were first and foremost exceptional moments of encounter with the men and women who agreed to enter into them.

I am reminded of a very old article by Jay Haley, the strategic therapist heavily influenced by Milton Erickson. With his usual sarcasm, he wrote of "How to be a couple and family therapist while knowing practically nothing." His paradoxical advice could equally be addressed to any number of psychotherapists. His first piece of advice, basically, can be summarized as follows: above all, never divulge or demonstrate how you work. Hide behind codes of ethics, professional confidentiality or anything of this nature. If you do anything else you will only expose yourself to endless problems — you will reveal your incompetence, get criticized, lose your power or your charisma and so on.

Well, I am prepared to run all these risks because I think that it is only by being prepared to lose that we can go forward.

2-1

THE WOMAN WHO TOOK THINGS FOR GRANTED

J-M. *Well . . . what is present for you?*

What is present is what I take for granted. Taking for granted that I want to be here, doing this training . . . It's about that! And at this moment, surprise at this kind of taking for granted.

J-M. *In fact there is already something that you take for granted but I don't . . . Could you try to make me feel, make me understand, what, for you, is being taken for granted? What counts as being taken for granted?*

It's something I don't question!
It's like a kind of . . . There! I'm sitting here on my chair, that's taken for granted, you see! And in terms of the purpose of this training, it's taken for granted that I want to do that!
And I'm a bit surprised at it. I'm a bit . . . "Who does she think she is?!"

J-M. *So there is both something that is taken for granted AND a kind of critical judgment!*

Yes! This morning, when I saw everyone here, I thought: What am I doing here? This became a question whereas it wasn't questioned before. The others had to be there so that . . .

J-M. *You started the process of challenging what was taken for granted again?*

Yes, exactly! That's it, to come here as a client was good! Something I kind of took for granted!

J-M. *So you are naming certain things that are taken for granted, obvious things which seem to be organizing some of your life circum stances: doing this training, coming and sitting down on this chair . . . And then you start enquiring, and afterwards you start asking yourself about these things that you take for granted: "Hey, what am I doing here?"*

Yeah, yeah . . . afterwards . . . and, how can I put this, perhaps when I'm sit face to face with the other. You weren't there then! Or, suddenly in front of the group . . . well, yes! I'm doing this training!

J-M. *Yes. So, the other, that's the one who comes along and destroys what you take for granted?*

Uh, yes! Not destroys in the sense that . . . it's not going to kill me!

J-M. *I mean: that destroys what you think of as obvious?!. . . And at that moment, what is happening? You say: "it was taken for granted that I would come and sit down" and a few seconds later: "Hey, what am I doing here?" You're in the presence of another . . .*

Yes, that's it! As soon as I started talking to you, it wasn't about what I took for granted any more! It was more . . . anxiety, that's putting it too strongly . . . let's say this feeling of tightness I used to get.

J-M. *"It wasn't any more?" Or "it was more?"*

It wasn't that any more, once I started talking, you see?
The same thing just now after I let the others do the talking, the tightness in my chest: "What am I doing here?" And then I started talking. It wasn't really taken something taken for granted any more, but it was easier.

J-M. *And so, by naming these kinds of taken for grantedness, and by naming these disruptions of the taken for granted (perhaps that's what we could call it?). . . .*

Yes.

J-M. . . . *and by telling me about it, is there something in particular that you want to make me understand, that you want to get across to me?*

I don't know. I think I want to get something across to you, but . . . maybe . . . I was going to say: get across to you how surprised I was! Yes! Tell you how much these breaks surprised me. . . .

J-M. *There, I'm wondering about the way I grasp what you are telling me . . . and I don't know quite where I am with all this! I am trying to . . . I am very focused on you rather than on what I feel . . . I'm not feeling very much, at the moment, and what is with me is: where is she going with this? Where do you want to go with this? What are you looking for?*

Well, there's nothing obvious!
(Laughter)

J-M. *(Laughing) Well, there you are!*

It's not taken for granted to me any more! I don't know where I'm going! The taken for granted is no longer taken for granted! I am — lost would be putting it too strongly — I feel . . . that I'm kind of worried . . .
You see, that reminds me, it comes back to me with the word 'lost' . . . I was organizing my trip to get here, I don't like flying, I'm a bit of a wuss, so I was going by rail. That's a taken

for granted thing for me, going by rail, I do it a lot! But there's a moment when I realize that it worries me, it makes me anxious, I feel a bit lost before I go, for the two days before. And then, last night, when I went through the last barriers and the train was there . . . there was something obvious about being there! There was something like that, feeling lost and finding something obvious!

J-M. *What I seem to be getting is that for you there's a kind of play off between what you take for granted and what is a surprise! Be tween astonishment, something that comes in the form of a break, and an almost basic functioning where there is no questioning: it is self evident!*
And so for me the question that arises is at what point and in what way do you make your choices?

(Silence) I'm looking for a get-out here!
I was going to say: how I am acted on sometimes . . .
How do I make my choices? . . .
(Silence)
I am thinking about the way I choose my clients. There are some, and with some, it's taken for granted. Well, so, we begin the therapy. With others, there's surprise! So in that case there is excitement but also fear . . . And I might tend to say: Oh, I don't get on with that one . . . And at the same time, they are the ones who give me . . .

J-M. *I'm going over what's just happened here for a minute. When I ask you the question about how you make choices, at that moment you state, you become aware that you are looking for a 'get out.' What is happening at that moment? Do you think that my question arouses anxiety?*

Of course I was escaping! It wasn't entirely conscious, but . . .

J-M. *What was it about my question that was troubling?*

Your question takes me back to . . . something really huge? 'How do you make your choices'!!!? Yes, it's the 'hugeness'!

J-M. *You didn't know how to take it . . .*

Yes, yes . . .

J-M. *If we try to make the question more specific, for example by looking at it alongside what's happening now: coming in and sitting down, that was something taken for granted . . .*

Yes!

J-M. *And you said, a few minutes later, that before I came and took my turn sitting in the armchair, something taken for granted turned into surprise, astonishment, 'What am I doing here?' A break in the taken for granted!*

So was it at that precise moment that the issue of choice could be raised?

Yes. I thought, choosing to be your client, that's something I take for granted. It's strange, I'm living this like something that is obvious for me, as if it was a sort of hyper-obviousness!

J-M. *Yes, clearly, the first phase, when it was taken for granted, you could say that there was no question of choice.*

No, because I was acted upon, actually!

J-M. *OK. And then? 'Ah! What am I doing here?' Maybe it was at that moment that . . .*

. . . that I could choose!

J-M. *Yes, that you could face up to a choice!*

Yes, but I was going to say, it's too late!

J-M. *Ah!*

(Laughs) It's too late! Here I am!

J-M. *You trapped yourself?*

Uh, yes! . . .

J-M. *What's happening now, what are you feeling right now?*

I'm thinking about fear, you know? I think that actually I'm a very fearful person, and it's as if my taken-for-granted (That's what I call it, hey?) was taking me to places where I wouldn't have gone if I'd have thought about it!

What's going to happen with Jean-Marie? . . . I would not have gone!!!

J-M. *Could we say that taking something for granted is your way of not looking?*

Yes, maybe that's it!
. . . and in fact, of not choosing!

J-M. *And so you use it as a way of adjusting so as to avoid fear?*

Yes, I'm someone who has a real fear of heights. I was thinking, as you were speaking, I saw myself like on a high wire: I have to go forward and . . . well, that's life!

J-M. *So? Are you interested in going on a little further together?*

Oh yes!

J-M. *So, in order to come and sit in this chair, you called on something taken for granted. So was there a fear? And that stopped you from . . . How could I make you afraid?*

That's a big question! . . .

That should be rather: how can you make me less and less afraid! How can I manage to see how you make me less and less afraid! Last time, I ran off, I remember our last interview! No, I didn't run off, but something bothered me!

J-M. *What I am finding out is that there may be unfinished situations . . .*

I don't know what you mean by 'unfinished.' I was going to check instead that I wasn't there any more.

J-M. *The previous situation being unfinished . . .*

No, no, it was finished! Because I didn't walk out in the middle of the interview and not see you again! I don't really know what happened. It was a mini training session, and I left, that evening, I wasn't well, and then we worked again next day. Unfinished maybe, but in any case, I wanted to finish off something!

J-M. *So now what you take for granted consists of confronting fear and going a step further, coming out of the taken for granted to see where you have got to?*

Yes.

J-M. *But in any case I don't quite see too clearly what I do to make you afraid!*

(She laughs) I don't take you for granted! (Laughs)

J-M. *I don't quite know what that might mean, being taken for granted! I've never been taken for granted, even by myself! (Laughter)*

I'm getting slightly hardened, you see, it's . . . something like a fight that might happen between you and me.

J-M. *When you imagine this battle, this fighting . . . what's it over?*

About not agreeing!

J-M. *About?*

Off the top of my head: about Gestalt therapy, for example! The aim wouldn't be to disagree, but my being ABLE to disagree! It's not very clear . . . What I'm thinking here is not necessarily about 'not agreeing,' the actual aim is not to disagree but to be able to disagree.

J-M. *I'm not sure I understand. Do you mean that what seems to be important to you is that you should have the option of disagreeing with me and for this to be recognized?*

The aim is not to be against you.

J-M. *It's neither being for nor being against, but you being able to exercise your difference, and this being accepted? . . .*

I was moved . . . I was touched to see how your eyes began to sparkle . . .

Yes, yes! (Laughs)

J-M. *. . . when you thought we could have this kind of relationship.*

Yes, yes, that touches me too!
Already I can see you better! You're more . . . perceptible!

J-M. *And then you were talking about fear earlier on, that could be something like . . . the fear of . . . affirming your difference from me?*

Yes, initially, but it's more about the fear of not knowing how to live it, or to explain my position.

J-M. *Fear of not being able to 'hold on'?*

Yes, yes! (Laughs) Yes! I'm so glad! I'm so glad! (Silence)

J-M. *. . . Can you say anything?*

My thoughts are whirling around! What I'm glad about is . . . it's about . . . because in fact, staying within what is obvious is a bit like being acted on! Well, that makes me do some things that are OK, because this, for example, this is good. But at the same time, it's . . .

And at the same time, what I'm glad about, it's being able to do it with full awareness, with my eyes wide open!

J-M. *So is there something you would like to assert now, in full awareness?*

To you!?

J-M. *To me and also to the group.*

To you, what I can assert is that I feel alive, and this isn't anything I take for granted, because I FEEL really alive!

J-M. *And this is something created in this encounter?*

Yes!

J-M. *Maybe to finish up, following on from what you were talking about, would it be good, later on in the course of our work, if at some point I made you feel less alive, if you were able to do something? Able to say something about it?*

Oh yes!

J-M. *I'm saying this because this way of using what's taken for granted might also be a kind of by product of certain retroflections . . .*

Well, yes! (Bursts out laughing)

J-M. *Maybe this isn't the place to worry about the 'old' ones, but if we manage at least not to create new ones, might that be valuable?*

Yes, that might be a very good program for me, here with you, not to end up with more!

J-M. *OK? Shall we leave it at that?*

Yes!

2-2

I Don't Have the Words to Talk About Myself

J-M. *OK. Is there something that's present for you here?*

Uh, yes! There was something present here, just now, when I was trying to express . . . it's always the same thing, I have the same difficulty in communicating with words. I don't know how to put things into words. It's always complicated, convoluted, it's something that's been a problem for me for a long time, that I've had for a long time, which means I have to make great efforts. And every time I have something to say, or a dissertation to write . . . something goes and suddenly I can't communicate because I find it difficult to make myself understood. I was talking about it with someone and I was telling him that you managed to say what I wanted to say in one sentence, but me . . . oh-oh!!! (gestures) . . . so it's something that keeps happening!

J-M. *Is it something that you have known about yourself for a long time?*

It's something that I've known about myself for a long time and it's something that poisons my life and complicates it. And . . . well, that's what I wanted to say about it!

J-M. *And do you have the feeling that these words are more or less there in your head and that the problem you have is getting them out, or do you feel that you think without words, in a sense?*

Yes, I get the feeling that I think with words that aren't necessarily the right ones. I go off into . . . it's more like impressions . . . I get the feeling that it's impressions . . . more than a specific sentence! But actually it's not necessarily all that precise, the word I was going to use maybe doesn't have exactly the meaning it usually has. Things like that . . . As if I was more into some overall idea than something quite precise about what I normally want to say.

J-M. *What I assume, since you say that you've had this difficulty for a long time, is that you have already looked at the problem from all angles, thought about it, and tried to work out what was happening, to understand something about it, am I right?*

Yes but I don't think that . . . Yes, about putting into words, the problem I have with . . . speaking, the way I don't say things or I say things differently, yes, I've already turned that over in my mind, but . . . It's also to do with the fact that I have problems with . . . uh, with . . . with . . . what you might call "identification/ alienation," wanting to say too many things at the same time, yes . . . wanting to say too many things, not sorting them out properly, something like that . . .

J-M. *As if you had too much stuff that . . .*

. . . that was crowding to get out the door!

J-M. *(almost at the same time) . . . pushing to get out the door*

When I was a little girl at school, elementary school, they used to say to me "Turn your tongue round your mouth seven times before you speak!" As if everything was rushing . . .

J-M. *Do you feel that you have this problem when you are talking to me now?*

Yes, because I get confused while I'm talking! I mean, I have a problem speaking . . . and also . . . thinking! I can't do both at the same time! Yes, it's difficult!

J-M. *Do you feel that . . . you need to think first and then speak?*

Yes! That's why I need to be by myself . . . then I can think and start over in order to communicate. But doing both at the same time, that's too much! So it's really slow!!!

J-M. *Do you feel, when you talk to me about these difficulties, do you feel that you are sending me a message that isn't clear, that's confused, and that I might well find it difficult to grasp what you're saying?*

No, because I'm telling you! I'm telling you things that I've been able to think about, things that I've been able to go over several times! So I can just about put it into the right words!

J-M. *You've had practice! And when you've had practice, like now, that's OK!*

Yeah! . . . Like now, I can make myself understood!

J-M. *So, it's when it's something new . . . ?*

Yes . . . or if there's some emotion!

J-M. *Or if there's some emotion?*

Yes, something like . . . not necessarily emotion but when something happens . . . uh! . . . the "id" being activated! Or something that comes from outside and starts to happen, well then I get overcome with . . . what's happening and I find it hard to maintain a distance.

J-M. *What makes you think that this difficulty you're having may need a psychotherapist's attention?*

Because I know that obviously there's something that's stuck someplace, that means . . . as if there was some development in the brain's logical maturation process or something . . . that hasn't happened. So I feel that there's something that stopped somewhere. Or maybe! . . . I also think that I just function differently! I function more with impressions, for example when it comes to memory, I don't remember . . . I've done . . . a number of things that I don't remember, but I remember impressions very well. Maybe I function more at that level and that's why I find it hard to . . . express myself in other ways! In fact maybe it has its useful side, but in everyday life it's a handicap. Maybe both, what I think is, I've developed like that, maybe because I found it hard the other way.

J-M. *Would you be prepared to try and tell me something about the impressions that you've been able to form since we've both been involved in this seminar?*

Uh, obviously, nothing comes to mind, right away the . . . like that, obviously nothing occurs to me! But if I try to . . . tell you something about . . . what comes to mind most, it's more things about how I was, how I experienced things, how I felt, that kind of thing . . .

J-M. *Would you like to try and say something about that?*

In the beginning, I was really . . . well, calm, and because of the place, I was very aware of the way that the place is . . . arranged, the materials, the doors and windows, the materials, how it's designed and so on, I was very happy with all that. And then as we go on, I feel a flood of personal things, of emotions, of things that make me messy, that stop me from being completely here. And then I also realized . . . just how much I ought . . . I was moving towards . . . certain choices . . . which were not going to be easy for me . . . and that are absolutely necessary. To give you a picture, at home, I like it to be . . . kind of . . . I can't find the words, the words aren't coming to me here . . . No! I can't find the words! Well, I like it to be a certain way . . . the word that comes to mind is 'pure' but that's not the right word . . . and then I add a whole lot of stuff. Two years later, it's . . . It's actually cozier, more all that, but . . . It's what I have to do when I go back! So, it's about something like that, which makes me . . . so I'm glad I realized that, but at the same time I'm . . . it's not comfortable!

J-M. . . . *When you tell me about your relationship with words, the difficulty you have in starting to speak, when you tell me about the example you give now, about your home, I have the impression that in both cases you are talking about compromise . . .*

Yes (*in a tearful voice*), and you see, that makes me sad! It's painful . . . yes . . . and it's also . . . I can't do anything else for the time being! At the moment, I let myself be swamped by all this clutter, even in my everyday life!

J-M. *So in both cases what you experience is something that stops you getting things out, expressing yourself, speaking out . . .*

And I'd even go so far as to say, it stops me . . . succeeding! (silence)

J-M. *What you make me think there, is that maybe there would be something disastrous about succeeding!*

Yes, I was just thinking that . . . that I didn't want to succeed. And that's exactly what I'm doing . . . I do all I can to not succeed! (silence)

J-M. *For example, imagine that you really do manage to put things into words . . . what might the consequence of that be . . . would it be serious . . . ?*

I think the consequences are sufficiently serious that I don't even want to . . . What I mean is, up to now I've never been in a position to even think about it. It's always been something impossible. So I can't even begin to imagine it . . . It's closed off!

J-M. *You close yourself off?*

I close myself off to such an extent that I don't feel any more! You see! I can't even say it to myself . . .

J-M. *Would you like me to tell you about an idea I've had? (She nods in agreement) I don't know if it's right! A few minutes ago, when I was talking to you about those two kinds of experience you have, the one with language and the other with your house, I linked them together with the word 'compromise.' And you then you were moved and the emotion you started to feel had some meaning for you. I also thought of another possibility . . . It seemed to me that what was happening at that time was the emotion because you were understood.*

(She smiles — silence)

J-M. *What's happening?*

No it's . . . it's something that . . . (she smiles, embarrassed) that . . . it's something that . . . it's . . . I think . . . it's something that I tend to . . . toward but at the same time, I don't like it! So I'm moving two ways at once.

J-M. *Wanting but being afraid?*

Yes, wanting and being afraid . . . what occurs to me is, it's kind of like heaven: it's something you can't even imagine! It's something completely . . . I'm like a little girl, things way beyond like . . . like Prince Charming, childish things!
And when I say this, I think: I'm being completely ridiculous. If I find it, that's not it, I'm making up a story . . . that's what comes to me at the same time.

J-M. *If I understand you right, you seem to have some kind of dream, an idealized ...*

Yes!

J-M. *... but "I mustn't even think about it!" ...*

Yes, but also, these aren't the sort of things you talk about: "you are understood!" uh ...

J M. Do you feel understood?

Yeah, well! (embarrassed laugh) I get the impression that with this I'm completely divided between a part of me that says 'Yes, of course you're understood' and another part that goes 'But actually, no, not at all!' It's confused as well!

J-M. *So at the same time there are aspects of your experience in which you feel received and understood, and aspects of yourself where you don't feel at all welcomed and understood ...*

It's more as if, if you like, as if there were something now ... because I've thought about it a bit ... as if there were something that I was dragging around! And especially this feeling of not being understood, I drag it around ... and I keep finding it ...

J-M. *And you hang on to it ...*

And I hang on to it!

J-M. *And you feed it . . .*

And I feed it!

J-M. *. . . by not finding the words which would enable you to be understood?!*

And that's what I don't want any more. And that's what I can't get away from!
(silence)

J-M. *What are you feeling, right now?*

Uh! What was I feeling just now? That I was, uh, astonished to be like that face to face with you, in your very compelling presence, very . . . uh, rooted, and so that was surprising to me to be there, opposite you, and to be uh . . . in general I always feel . . . I always feel that I'm in a strong position and (laughs) because you have a very strong presence and so I didn't feel that at all because I felt this force, this presence here.
The aura you have is three-dimensional, like a sculpture rather than a painting, much more . . . strongly drawn . . . (makes vigorous gestures) . . . other words too but I don't know . . .

J M. *I'm a bit lost here because I asked you what you were feeling . . .*

I realized that!

J-M. *. . . and you are talking about me more than about you!*

Because I was just . . . just . . . feeling this difference in . . . ways of being. The fact that you're there, that you are as you are, means that I feel different.

J-M. *Are you telling me that you experience me as having some kind of strength, that there is some kind of power in my presence . . . ?*

Yes

J-M. *. . . and suddenly, you don't need to feel strong?*

Maybe, yes!

J-M. *Have you trained yourself to be strong?*

I don't know if I've trained myself, but I had to be!

J-M. *You had to be! And here?*

And here, I didn't have to be! And so . . . there you are!

J-M. *So then if it's possible for you to be a slightly fragile, flexible Véronique . . . how do you think people will hear you and under stand you? Can you be heard and understood?*

Ah yes ... I have come to realize over the last few days that I was perceived very differently ... and probably I seemed like ... and that gave me a sweet feeling. And that's something new! And I feel a lot better. There's a way to go ... but I'm a lot better!

J-M. *And how is it, feeling like that?*

Oh, it's ... it's really good! (silence)

J-M. *What's really surprising is that it doesn't seem to make you stumble over your words!*

No, because it's reassuring! So I don't stumble over words! But it makes me ... as I was saying just now, it's more as if ... I don't know, it's not clear ... if you like, when I don't manage to express myself, it's when I want ... when I want to recount something!

J-M. *I am sensitive, right now, to something that's happened sev eral times during our conversation, that is ... when you're con fronted with the difficulty of putting what you want to say to me into words, at that moment you have a speech mannerism and you say 'if you like'!*

Do I?

J-M. *But it's not me who likes anything!*

I know I'm starting to look away! But this 'if you like' . . . I'd never noticed it before!

J-M. *Could we explore the idea that this difficulty might have something to do with what the other person wants, or what you think they want?*

Mmm . . .

J-M. *Does this make sense to you?*

In principle . . . it's really hard because I'm going to tell you stuff that I think I know about myself . . . To tell you that I know that in principle I'm going to comply with what the other person wants . . . but that's telling you things that aren't happening right now. Because what's happening now, it's nothing, I don't know any longer!

J-M. *It's nothing?*

Yes . . . I don't know now . . . it's nothing . . .

J-M. *You say: I accept that it's nothing! Or do you have to plunge into the reservoir of . . .*

Yes of . . . what I know, what I might have felt in other situations where I was able to lean on something . . . This nothing,

it's that . . . the only thing possible was nothing. The only way out was in nothing. There, if I'm honest, that's it. If I remain how I am, I can't say anything to you because . . . I think I've developed the habit, for a long time now, that when something like that happened, when somebody asked me something like you did just now, uh, well . . . my reply in order to . . . perhaps not doing what the other person wanted but in any case being comfortable with myself, was nothing. Because that way I can disguise myself, I don't compromise myself. It's clear to me, I don't know if it's clear to you?
No?

J-M. *Uh . . . I am trying to turn round in my head various possible meanings in what you are saying . . . and it made me think, among other possibilities, that when you are called upon, implicitly or ex plicitly, to speak by the other, there might be something that you say for yourself, as one possibility, and then there's something that you say because the other expects it, which is the other possibility. So does that mean that either you say nothing, or else you say something in a confused way?*

Absolutely! (very moved) That's exactly right! . . . yes, yes . . . And the confused words, the two things that happen, that image is completely right. Yes, yes . . . And at that point, everything crashes! And that's the only issue, otherwise I don't exist! At that moment I withdraw! So whatever I might say, I know that I've withdrawn!

J-M. *I can see that you're touched . . . what kind of emotion are you experiencing?*

It's very difficult . . . as soon as you ask me, the mechanism starts to operate . . . I am moved, and I don't know what to attach it to . . .

J-M. *OK! Let's take the risk! Imagine that I WANT you to tell me something specific, about this emotion of yours, OK?*

What automatically comes to mind, you mean, for me?

J-M. *No. In asking the question, 'What are you feeling now, is there some emotion present?' I am asking you to imagine that there is an answer that I am expecting from you.*

Uh! I don't know you well enough to be sure . . .

J-M. *Go on! Risk it!*

Uh! What you expect from me . . . uh, I think you are . . . There, you see, I'm trying to see according to . . . therapeutic stuff, blah blah . . .

J-M. *Set your intuition going!*

Well, uh . . . What comes to mind? What was the question you asked?

J-M. *Oh, it was just: what was the emotion that you were experiencing at that time?*

Yes, in relation to the fact that the two things get confused . . . uh . . . uh . . . I'll tell you . . . what comes to mind are all the psychoanalytic clichés . . .

J-M. *Go on!*

No but . . . that's not what you expect from me!

J-M. *It doesn't matter! It doesn't matter . . . because we're just exploring the idea of projection here! Feel free to go there!*

All right, bearing in mind that I don't think that everything . . . (laughs) . . . So it's about the relationship I had with my mother and about . . . But you don't really expect that? . . . You're not that concerned? It's an automatic tic! I know that! You see? . . .

J-M. *So, can we assume then that that isn't what I wanted to hear at all, agreed?*

Yes, yes . . .

J-M. *. . . But it could be what you want to say to me!*

Ah! . . . Yes, that's it! Because it is not false either! Maybe, yes, because that has its place too!

J-M. *OK! So, anyway, there's this conflict again between what Jean Marie is supposed to expect . . .*

And since I don't know what that is . . .

J-M. *You don't know what it is but . . . as it doesn't coincide with what you yourself would want to say (gesture of knocking hands together and letting them fall) you don't say anything!*

Yes, it's the other way round but it's the same thing, absolutely! (laughs) It works both ways!

J-M. *Would you be prepared to do a little experiment, to tell me about a psychoanalytic something or other which is important to you right now?*

Yes, I think so . . . if you like . . .

J-M. *If I like?*

Oh! (laughs) Yes, which is important to me, the extent to which the relationship I had with my mother was, and still is very much present, and it still poisons me! But not her! . . .

J-M. *In terms of . . . her expectations or . . . ?*

In terms of how our relationship was constructed!

J-M. *And how would you describe it?*

I'd describe it as a kind of . . . whew . . . fusion, yes, in fact there was nothing else, no support at all, no protection. And THAT! That's something that poisons me, that I drag around with me!

J-M. *Fusion of words, fusion of individuals . . .*

Yes, fusion of people, fusion of words, or even no words, and at the same time, left to my own devices!

J-M. *And is it good for you to tell me about an idea like that, that you don't think I subscribe to?*

(laughs) Is it good? I can't answer you! I don't have any way of knowing . . .

J-M. *Do you find it good, do you find it pleasant to express an idea that you think I don't subscribe to?*

I don't have any feelings . . .

J-M. *You are cutting out right now?*

I'm cutting out!

J-M. *You would rather not know?*

That's right (laughs) That's right! In any case the result is that I'm incapable of saying what . . .

J-M. *Do you think it's something that I can receive?*

Yes, I think you can receive it, yes! (silence)

J-M. *Well, maybe we'll try coming back down to earth gently . . . Is there anything that you would like to finish, to add to what we have been able to say?*

No, what is with me is the image of clutter, the image of words that get mixed up, and of 'working both ways,' that's something that is really there for me. Thank you.

2-3

I Am Tense with Despair

J-M. *You were expressing various feelings before you came and sat down here . . .*

Yes, that I don't know if I'm more afraid or if I'm more ashamed? I don't know.

J-M. *And what is most present now?*

I'm going to relax, I'm going to relax, I'm going to relax . . .

J-M. *Do you mean that you're tense, that you're tense, that you're tense? . . .*

No, I don't feel tense!

J-M. *So, what's the point of relaxing?*

(laughter)

(Deep sigh) There are these ideas that go through my head . . . past reminiscences.

J-M. *Do you mean that in your system of representation, coming and sitting down here should be a source of tension, but that you don't feel any tension?*

(This session is taking place abroad. The translator automatically repeats my question in French instead of translating it. She realizes this and asks me to repeat what I have just said so she can translate it. Instead, I make a mistake too and start to translate what I said previously into Spanish. General hilarity. Then I repeat my question in French).

Yes. I think I can be more or less relaxed. I wanted to work with you when you came to my town and I talked to my therapist about it . . .

J-M. *So you are here to finish something that was unfinished, a frustration that's been unresolved since the first time we met . . . ?*

It's really since yesterday that I've felt it was possible to work together! It was clearer yesterday, more possible, more realistic. And that's the reason why I'm here today.

J-M. *And do you feel you want to work on something specific?*

(silence) What's been going round in my head is the work I did with another therapist. How do I take control of my need . . . ? I'm forty years old and with an inner child. I think we could talk about a feeling of abandonment. This is something important I feel inside.

J-M. *You feel that the theme of abandonment is one you think about a lot. As if you were abandoned? Is that what you want to tell me?*

Important, no! Right now, lately, I don't know what to do about this. I don't know how to think about it again. It's something old, hidden, and with the work that I did with the other therapist, it's something that came out . . .

J-M. *But . . . could you tell me a bit more about it, because when you talk about abandonment, I'm not quite sure what you're talking about. You also talk about your work with another therapist, but, again, I'm not sure what you you're talking about.*

I think I'm talking about despair.

J-M. *I don't know what the difference is between despair in general and YOUR despair in particular. What is your despair like?*

I don't know if there is a difference: I haven't taken responsibility for mine. I'm in the process . . . of taking responsibility for it.

J-M. *I don't understand.*

Mine didn't exist.

J-M. *I don't understand.*

It didn't exist because I didn't take responsibility for it. For despair in general . . .

J-M. *And what about your own? Do you think you could try to . . . not necessarily explain it to me, but make me feel what your own despair is like?*

(silence) It's impossible to breathe, it stays in here (holds head in hands). It's negative ideas. It provokes reactions that I don't understand . . . I see this as an overarching theme. It's a blind spot that it's very difficult to look into, it's somewhere I don't want to look . . .

J-M. *Would you like us to look at it together?*

(silence, takes deep breaths with some difficulty while looking at me very intensely) What good would that do? . . . Actually, yes!

J-M. *I am aware of . . . how I receive your verbal responses, and also your nonverbal responses. When I asked you "what is your own despair like?" I saw that you looked up at the ceiling. And broke off*

visual contact with me for quite a while. And I realize that I re
ceived that as if you were saying: "My own despair is that I can't
form a bond with anyone, I can't find support in a relationship
with another person, my despair is about being forced to go off some
where else, all alone." And when I said "Would you like us to look at
it together?", at the word "together" your eyes never left mine. And
it seems to me that there was an emotion there too, a little . . . and
very soon words came along and smothered all that . . .
(silence)
What is happening here, what are you feeling now?

(silence) I feel as if . . . I'm understood. I was thinking . . . What is this theoretical stuff you're talking about! But
it's theoretical stuff that's very, very true . . . Understood . . . I
feel as if I'm understood. I feel brilliantly understood. I don't
know that you have to be brilliant to be understood but . . .

Interpreter (in French): I don't think the group can hear you
too well . . .

J-M: *(to her) Maybe you should speak louder?*

Interpreter: Well . . . and what about him? (Points to patient)

Client: What's she saying?

J-M. *She says that maybe the group can't hear us. (the interpreter*
translates) And that we should speak louder.

(He slumps back in his chair and pulls a face)

J-M. *You don't like the idea, huh?*

(Moves closer to me) No! (Laughing, mimes speaking into a megaphone and whispers something inaudible. I copy his gesture and laugh with him). It's one thing to invite you, but inviting thirty people, no!

J-M. *Are you talking about your need for intimacy, for closeness?*

(Silence. He looks at me very intensely, puts out his hand and takes hold of mine. Then he completes the gesture with his both hands. We stay together for a long while in silence. He breathes out deeply)

J-M. (We let go our hands). *Are there any words, even confused ones, which come to mind?*

(A few seconds of silence) Thank you. It's kind of . . . I've gotten past something . . . but I feel ridiculous saying that. But . . . super . . . but gotten past what? But I've worked with you!

J-M. *And is that what's ridiculous? I don't understand what you experience as ridiculous?*

I think it's ridiculous that anyone should say anything to me because I've worked with you. That's nothing to do with it. (He strokes my arm lightly in an affectionate gesture). That's nothing to do with the good feeling, the pleasure of being with someone.

J-M. *And what's that about?*

About having successfully, in inverted commas, worked with you. I find myself saying both "That's good, I've worked with Jean-Marie" and also maybe, the most important thing that's happened for me, is to do with intimacy, my soli . . . my solitude . . . and my despair. (Silence)

J-M. *I get the feeling that at the moment there are a lot of things going through your mind. As if there was a kind of interior dia logue.*

Yes, the words that won't come out, these are things of mine that I have to sort out. Things of mine but that I've shared with you.

J-M. *But here, you are with me. Even when you're with me, I get the feeling that at times you would rather talk to yourself than talk to me.*

(Nods in agreement)

J-M. *It's a good way of staying alone!*

It's been like that for a long time.

J-M. *Have you been thinking for a long time that you are the only person capable of understanding you? And you are the only person who can receive you?*

I suppose I must have thought that at one time! And I think about what I could have done when I came to the conclusion that I had to be alone. And ever since . . . and now I was paying attention to what I was doing and what has to come out in order to work . . . It's something quite different.

J-M. *And we might think that at one time, it was important, and maybe even essential, for you to be alone, necessary even. But per haps now you seem to be saying that's it not so necessary?*

(He nods his head for some time)

J-M. *Would it be risky for you to realize that your needs might change?*

No, no, no! No, no! I'm there! It's not purely intellectual, rather it's . . .

J-M. *It's also physical! I am paying attention to your mouth, which is nearly always open, as if you were trying to signal to me some kind of greed for contact with the world . . . So that as many things as possible can enter into you and . . . And that touches me strongly.*

Do you think we can stop now . . . or should we carry on for a while? Which is most meaningful for you?

We shouldn't carry on to the point of indigestion! There shouldn't be too much. Thank you.

J-M. *Is there something that you would like to say to finish off? You said "Thank you," is there . . .*

He fixes his gaze on a point on the wall behind me, and smiling I turn round in a theatrical way and look at the same point. (We both laugh). No, it's fine like that, thank you.

2-4

I'm Ashamed of Thinking Differently

I wanted to come because I feel overcome with shame, and so . . . I want to work on that! In fact, what is happening, when we are all talking together, often I want to say something but I don't say it because . . . uh . . . I often want to say things that don't fit with current thinking, what's being said. And that's something that happens with me a lot. What I mean is that I'm often . . . not in agreement with what's being said, and in fact I often think the opposite. And when that happens, either I storm the barricades and I get annoyed (makes aggressive gestures) and then afterwards I feel bad, or else I keep quiet! Well, actually it's changed a bit over the years, but it's still really strong. So I said a couple of things but when that was still . . . that wasn't so different from what people were saying . . .

J-M. *So you associate shame with the fact of showing that you're different . . . ?*

Yes, that's right! Differentiating myself, revealing that I'm different. And that's something I feel very bad about, so uh . . .
And then, physically, I start to tremble and I can hardly breathe any more.

J-M. *Could you try to make me feel more clearly how, when you confront your difference and your need to affirm it that gives rise to shame?*

Yeah, what I said just now that I start to tremble and find it hard to breathe, it's not when I refrain from speaking, it's when I imagine speaking . . . and that's when I feel shame! And it often happens like that.

J-M. *And so, what is that allows you to observe, to identify, what you are feeling at that moment as shame . . . and not fear . . . anxiety or something else?*

I thought for a long time that it was fear, but now I am coming to realize that perhaps it was shame. I don't know, really, but for a long time I believed that I was in a state of terror! That's what I believed!

J-M. *You used to think that and now you don't think that any more!? . . .*

Well, I don't know, in fact! It seems to me that shame is rather . . . that seems right to me!

J-M. *What kinds of feelings and what kind of thoughts come to you in those moments, in those moments what you are describing?*

Things like: people are going to judge me, I'm not going to be up to it, I am going to have another attack of nerves, people will think I'm crazy again, I still have a problem, you see?

J-M. *Mmm! That is, you have some kind of terrifying expectation about what will happen . . .*

Yes.

J-M. *. . . and as you describe it to me now, that makes me think that of fear, of fear of having to experience shame!*

Mmm, yes, that's possible. While you were talking, I was thinking . . . there was one sentence that came through very strongly, that is, people won't like me! Underneath there is all that . . . So in order for people to like me, I hide myself, I stay in the background, I don't move around too much . . . It's true.

(silence) It's true that I don't often blush, for example. But there is really something that happens, I start to tremble, I start to feel bad, maybe that's something that precedes shame? Fear?

J-M. *Do you have in mind times, occasions when that happened during the hours that we've spent together, in this seminar?*

Of course! All the time I'm going like this (mimes going forward) then I . . . (mimes retreating)

J-M. *So what worries you is the fact that we are looking at you?*

Yes. I don't know if it's because of you all looking at me but I feel as if I'm not in the same movie, I'm somewhere else, I can't get in, something like that, so then I make a big production out of it: "Oh, all that, it's no use, it's not important, it's only theories . . . you can say one thing and then say the opposite, and it's all in vain! . . ." Or else I think: "Oh well, I've moved on, I'm not going to storm the barricades for all that, I'm calmer now, more serene" . . .

J-M. *You downplay the importance of what happens . . .*
I felt addressed when you said: "This has happened, this happens here, this happens often, I push myself forward (imitates her previous movement) then I withdraw (likewise)." I felt addressed because I do not perceive these movements by you, and so I cannot support them.

Mmm, mmm! Yes, of course . . .

J-M. *This movement forwards that you describe, was it an actual physical movement?*

Oh no! I know how to do it! I know how to adapt and disappear . . . And at the same time . . . I am bitterly aware of it . . . but, well!

J-M. *But, does it suit you when I let you disappear?*

No, but when it happens I can still say things. I've learned to say things, to keep in the swim of things, by sharing, like that . . . without needing to fit in with other people, and I take a good deal of pleasure in that, but sometimes I daren't go there . . .

J-M. *So, how have I indicated to you, because I can only speak for myself, not on behalf of all the other people here, what signal might I have sent you . . . that, if you manifested your difference, I would not like you any more?*

Yes, that's true, I have asked myself the same question, because I feel different here to how I do during a supervision: where I have begun to gain confidence and dare to say things, And here . . . it's true that I feel different, I feel I have less confidence. There's the group, there's the place, which is different, and also . . . and it's true that I had the feeling that there was some kind of coldness in you. It's normal, we're in training, all that . . . but it's true that I haven't felt as confident. It's true that there are several things involved: I'm not from around here, I'm not from this school, and it's true that I've been destabilized by your way of working, I did tell you one time . . . All that, means that . . . (makes gestures of withdrawal)

J-M. *Can you tell me a bit more about how I've destabilized you?*

When I've said something . . . sometimes, you haven't really picked up on it, or you've gone in another direction! And then other little signs like that, they have a big effect on me!

J-M. *These are signs that you take to be . . . signs of lack of love?*

Right away, yes! But although I realize that I'm making too much of it, that's still how I feel!

J-M. *OK, maybe you're making too much of it, but at the same time we can see that there is some basis for this.*

Oh no! I realize that!

J-M. *So I amplify your insecurity?*

Yes, yes! That's true! (silence)

And I'm thinking too that I couldn't stand it if you were really nice all the time, really like (embracing gesture) . . .

J-M. *Might that mean that you are asking me to find a happy medium? I realize that you have used things that have happened between you and me in the group to construct a whole scenario!*

Yes!

J-M. *And I suppose that your whole life experience features in this scenario . . .*

Yes, of course!

J-M. *But at the moment, the important thing for me is how you and I can create the condition that are safe enough for you to be able to follow your own way, at your own pace, including with your scenarios . . . but let's be clear about it! Because, if I understand it, what I am encouraging you to do is to come back to a mode that you are only too familiar with: retroflection!*

Yes! (silence) What I am thinking is that it is not so much retroflection that bothers me, it's not having the pleasure of sharing things with others.

J-M. *That's an outcome of retroflection!*

Yeah! Retroflection, I don't care, that's how it is! But it takes away the pleasure of sharing. I like sharing my ideas, and I like saying things that are maybe not run-of-the mill. I am depriving myself of enjoyment here!

And what I would like too, would be not to be so focused, not be constantly decoding these little signs of how you are reacting, not being insecure all the time . . . about what you might . . . about whether you like me or not . . . If you like me as I am, whether you're in a good mood or a bad mood, but not let it bother me . . . (signs indicating 'underneath')

J-M. *All these little signals, you use them to construct . . . a system to avoid accepting this enjoyment.*

Yeah!

J-M. *So for me the question that now arises is: what would be so catastrophic about accepting this enjoyment?*

Uh, I don't know! (laughs) (Silence)
That people might resent it, I don't know . . .

J-M. *Imagine that things happen here that allow you to connect with this pleasure. And in the relationship with me and with all of us . . .*

I am thinking about my Protestant family background: it was not done to take any pleasure! You had to be a bit gray, a bit dull, stay in the background . . . Enjoyment was a bad thing! And especially for a woman to say things . . . Because my family is very Protestant! There were a lot of pastors, and that's quite something! I'm not sure if it's just about that, but . . .

J-M. *Do you put yourself in a position, even now, of obedience to this family convention? And you fade out any opportunity to have a pleasurable relationship with words?*

Yes, yes! (silence) While you're talking I have images of my grandparents' home (laughs) It's very austere!

J-M. *And so, how would that be if you had enjoyable relationships with me, with us? Would that be betraying your family?*

That might be something to do with it because even now I'm still rebelling against my family. My parents are no longer alive, but for a year now I've cut myself off from the rest of the family because I just can't stand how I am constantly having to show them that I don't live the same way, that I'm not like them . . . And they don't understand, so I've broken off with them completely! So there might be something like that! I'm really still reacting!

J-M. *Yes! But at the same time you are explaining to me that when you're here, you're not reacting against your family!*

That's why I'm reacting, because actually it affects me very strongly! And the fact that not following their conventions, that's a disaster for them: for them it means I'm not well . . . they don't understand!

J-M. *They judge you negatively?*

I feel I'm exhausting myself!

J-M. *Might that mean that if you present yourself here as being different, out of line, there's a risk that we might, that I might, be scornful?*

Yes, yes, it's possible!

J-M. *So we're going back to the issue of shame that you raised at the beginning!*

Yes! (silence) I feel on the verge of tears . . . I know how to retroflect them . . . but I'm telling you! (laughs)

J-M. *I can know this but I can't see it.*

There, you didn't notice! Huh?

J-M. *I saw it, I saw the beginnings of a wanting . . . that means that I can know this but not see it.*

Did you see it?

J-M. *Yes!*

Before I told you about it?

J-M. *At the same time!*

Oh OK! . . . Yes!
Yes! It isn't done to cry, to show pleasure, it's not done
to . . . That's how you have to be! Like a man, in fact! But as
for me, I don't really feel ashamed! And that's the tragic part,
because I'm always . . . stopping myself from saying, from
showing . . .

J-M. *I have this fantasy: could we think of something that you*
might be telling me or showing me that you think is 'out of line,'
and that you would be prepared to risk?

(She laughs)

J-M. *What is happening when I suggest this to you?*

(silence) It seems impossible! Something really out of line? A
little out of line . . . OK! But really out of line, that seems impossible?

J-M. *So, you're staying within the norm?*

In fact I'm pretending to stay within the norm!

J-M. *You know, a pretense that lasts throughout your life, that's not so different from your actual life!*

Yes, that's true, but not everybody knows that! Well done!

J-M. *So it's more important for you to appear to be staying within the norm?*

Well, no! Not at all! But that's what I do . . . I would like not to . . . but that's what I do! It's a question of survival!

J-M. *Even if you felt safe enough to experiment?*

No! I absolutely have the fantasy that if I say certain things you will get the idea that I'm dangerous . . . that I'm really fooling around!

J-M. *So?*

I REALLY don't want to!

J-M. *I can't help thinking that what you are telling us is that you think you're dangerous and that you're fooling around!*

No but sometimes I'm so much the opposite that I . . . I should never say things like that! But I don't think I'm a monster at all! But I have the feeling that people will judge me!

J-M. *When you're within the norm and therefore not dangerous, is it the only way to stay lucid?*

Yes! (laughs)

J-M. *OK!*

It's still something I have!

J-M. *And so you're telling me that here, we encourage people to stay within the norm?*

No, not at all. We are trying . . . to share things, but . . . I think that unconsciously there is this really strong thing, which is part of my life history! No, on the contrary, I'm actually glad to hear certain things that I don't hear elsewhere, a way of talking and conceptualizing certain things. Of course, this is theoretical, there is no truth . . . etcetera. But it still makes me react like that! (silence)

J-M. *I am experiencing a rather strange feeling: that is that there is something of yourself that you let me see, that you have also let me see in other circumstances, and there is also something about you that I KNOW, because you tell me and I have no reason not to believe you, which is that you are not how you appear. You think that you are out of line, and if you showed yourself for what you are people would consider you crazy or dangerous . . . I know this! I know this because you are telling me now, and you have said it before. I have all this information. And all this information makes up a whole (gestures of bringing together) I can't say: I rely on what I see, or rather, I rely to what I hear . . . AND at the same time I realize that my feelings are . . . contaminated by this mixture!*

Meaning?

J-M. *Meaning that although you tell me: "if you knew who I really was, you would run away fast!" I have no desire to run away fast! Yet you're telling me that you're some kind of horror!*

Well, not to that extent! (bursts out laughing) Horror?!!!

J-M. *Yes, my expression, not yours!*

Yes, but I see that you're getting at. You mean that I might be, I could be, dangerous . . . , crazy . . . ! And that doesn't make you want to run away? Really?

J-M. *Uh, no!*

Ah ha! (sounding surprised)

J-M. *Do you want me to run away?*

No! not at all. No, that's actually what I'm afraid of!

J-M. *So what function does it have for you to give me this warning? Because if you tell me: "I'm crazy, but I don't show it, I'm dangerous but I don't show it," if you give me this warning . . . what kind of game are you playing with me?*

I just want you to know who I am!

J-M. *Yes, but you don't want to show me!*

Maybe I'll show you later on! (laughs)

J-M. *So, this is a kind of intermediate, preparatory stage, you're testing the water, seeing if the water is warm enough to swim in?*

Sure, that's right, so you know who I am, that you don't run away, that you still like me, and so that I can have the confidence to swim later on! That kind of thing! Yes!

J-M. *So this is a kind of test that you're setting me, and I suppose the whole group?*

Yes, yes, that's right!

J-M. *Could we also understand what you are saying as: I would like it very much if you would give me some feedback, some sign that you are not going to run away if I show that I'm different, if I act in a way that I think might be diagnosed as some kind of craziness?*

Yes, yes! I've been thinking that I have a terrible foreign accent and I think to myself: they are going to laugh at me, and then I feel shame! (laughs)

J-M. *And this difference in accent, it's more . . . ?*

I find it amusing, in fact, as well as being a little ashamed of it. Some years ago, I lost my accent, and then I took it on again . . . I like that and it amuses me. But I still feel a little ashamed! Between shame and pleasure!

J-M. *And it's better not to feel pleasure? (somewhat provocatively)*

Ah! (laughs)

2-5

Looking like an Idiot?

J-M. *So! What is here for you now?*

My heart's beating . . . my hands are sweating. I'm finding it difficult to breathe . . .

J-M. *So what are these signs of, for you?*

That I'm agitated.

J-M. *Can you try to make me understand what you're anxious about?*

Because I don't know you. I feel all mixed up, everyone is looking at me, and I don't know what is going to happen.

J-M. *And when you're in an unknown place, with an unknown guy, with other people looking at you, it makes you anxious?*

Mmm mmm!

J-M. *And what are you anxious about?*

It's fear! Fear of looking ridiculous, of not doing things well, not being able to show that I'm intelligent . . .

J-M. *And these are situations that you're familiar with?*

Yes, if happens a lot! It happens to me a lot!

J-M. *And so you would rather not be in this type of situation a gain?*

I would like to be able to do things better. I do things badly and yes, I'd like to avoid that!

J-M. *And you don't think you're a ridiculous person, you think you're an intelligent person . . .*

Yes (laughs) kind of, yes!

J-M. *So does that mean that there is one side of you that you want to show and another side that you don't want to show?*

Yes, clearly! I like to play the clown, to be funny, but that doesn't fit with my "intelligent" side. I don't think you can be funny and intelligent at the same time. Be both a clown and serious.

J-M. *How did you learn to make this distinction?*

I don't know.

J-M. *Because apparently you think you are gifted in both ways.*

Yes. In my family I was the clown, I think.

J-M. *When you were the clown, did they think you were a little stupid?*

Yes! That's kind of the role I had. And I was left in peace like that!

J-M. *So there were advantages as well?*

Yes, yes!

J-M. *But here you're afraid of being stupid?*

Yes.

J-M. *And so you're making the choice not to be necessarily happy?*

Yes, yes! (laughs)

J-M. *I see a deep sigh . . . and also emotion.*

Yes, because I feel that you're giving me permission to do how I like.

J-M. *And you're touched to have this permission?*

Yes!

J-M. *Is this something you're not used to?*

Oh yes, yes!

J-M. *Can you tell me a little more about it?*

(silence) . . . No . . .

J-M. *What I am getting from what you are telling me now is that in order to be how you want to be, you need somebody's permission.*

Yes.

J-M. *I'm curious to know how you manage when nobody gives you permission . . . That's a deep sigh!*

I'm swallowing.

J-M. *But you're showing something.*

I'm nervous like this, but usually nobody sees it . . . I'm perspiring . . . I think it's the effort of swallowing, that's what makes me perspire.

J-M. *The irritation at not being able to show either of your two sides.*

Yes.

J-M. *So you disappear?*

Yes, I feel closed off, constrained . . .

J-M. *But at the same time you're telling me that feeling constrained and closed off is also more comfortable for you?*

It should be! But it isn't as comfortable as all that! I don't feel good but I'm used to it. I'm not too ill at ease.

J-M. *Are you telling me that you experience a kind of chronic but low level discomfort?*

Yes. I feel it here. (points to her stomach)

J-M. *Is that where you store it?*

Yes, it comes and goes, and my hands sweat. I don't realize it but sometimes that happens. I try not to take any notice of it. I am sitting down and I have a feeling in my stomach.

J-M. *What kind of feeling?*

Oppression.

J-M. *Is there something that feels oppressive to you in what is hap pening now?*

Yes. You, it's as if you were poking your finger into my stom- ach. I'm not used to it.

J-M. *Is it that . . . should I understand that I am acting toward you or behaving in a rather violent or intrusive way?*

(silence) I don't have that feeling physically. It's your words that affect me.

J-M. *And what are my words like?*

You make me pay attention to my sensations.

J-M. *And . . . ?*

And I realize what's happening and I don't like it.

J-M. *So I am doing something with you that you don't like.*

Yes, I don't like it.

J-M. *But you're not stopping me?!*

No, no! I realize that I'm not stopping you!

J-M. *So . . . I'm still torturing you?*

But I don't know how to stop you. I don't know if I should go away or what I should do to you!

J-M. *So you have a feeling . . . of ineffectiveness or impotence?*

(silence) I don't feel ineffective . . . but I think I let you do what you want. I have the resources to stop you. But I let you go on!

J-M. *So I haven't yet been sufficiently unbearable? I haven't yet gone too far?*

I can still stand it, yes!

J-M. *But at a certain point, you think you would be able to stop me?*

Yes, but it would probably be too late.

J-M. *I am really hearing what you are telling me, because you are telling me that I can upset you, even if I don't want to, but I can do something that hurts you, that hurts your stomach for example, and that you are very tolerant. And you can accept feeling bad for some time because of me. And I don't like that. I don't like knowing that I'm hurting you.*

I didn't know it was important to you.

J-M. *(Short silence) And I didn't know that it wasn't important to you. Feeling bad.*

I'm used to it. Not stopping, and the other person not knowing. And that's not important either!

J-M. *And it's OK like that!*

No, it's not OK like that! (laughs)

J-M. *You see, I can play the clown too!*

Yes!

J-M. *So how are we going to meet each other?* . . .

Through our hands (she puts out her hands, I do not take them) I only think without words . . .

J-M. *It's my words that are coming here . . . For you, violence and aggression come with words. With hands, there is much more soft ness, gentleness. You know this.*

Yes, it's words that hurt me. It's not often that a caress hurts me. Words resonate here (points to her ear), come in there and then come in here (points to her stomach).

J-M. *(I move forward a few inches) Can you imagine that there might be a way of touching each other with words without it being painful? . . .*

Mmm . . . I find it difficult to understand!

J-M. *This is something you're not used to?!*

Yes! yes . . .

J-M. *And I suppose . . . Just now, you spoke about the unknown as insecurity!*

(silence) It's strange because the tone of your voice and your eyes . . . don't hurt me. But when you moved nearer, I was afraid.

J-M. *So I can create a mixture of feelings in you: a mixture of secu rity and insecurity at the same time.*

Yes! If I hide your mouth (she lifts her arm and puts her hand like a screen between us) and I only see your eyes, I'm much calmer!

J-M. *The problem with my mouth is that it can talk?!!! Is that it?*

(She laughs) Yes! And draw closer through words.

J-M. *Are you asking me to keep my distance?*

Yes!

J-M. *(I lean back in my chair) Like that? Further?*

Yes. (She pulls her chair back a couple of feet)

J-M. *Ah! You would rather you pull back than me? It's always you who do all the work?*

Yes!!!

J M. So I'm the lord and master and you have to adapt! Protecting yourself, distancing yourself, coming nearer . . . you're the one who does all the work!

It's tiring but . . . yes!

J-M. *But I'm aware that you are a stranger to me as well. And it was you who took the step of coming to see me!*

Yes!

J-M. *I now realize, with hindsight, that it must have taken a good deal of courage on your part!*

(laughs) I wasn't alone!

J-M. *Where are they, your parents?*

(laughs)

J-M. Do you feel supported by the people who came with you?

Yes!

J-M. *I'm learning things about you little by little. Just now, you presented yourself as somebody who was alone, closed off, taking responsibility for everything . . . And now I find out that you are capable of looking for support!*

Yes. It would have been difficult for me to come by myself!

J M. We are going to stop now, but before we stop, is there any thing you would like to say?

I feel stupid (bursts out laughing), because I don't know if I've done things properly! But I know I've dared to do it and that the shame will go away!

J-M. *I feel a little wave of sadness when you say that. I didn't intend for you to feel stupid. But at the same time . . . I have mixed feelings, because I am thinking that if you really felt so stupid and so ashamed of being how you are . . . perhaps you wouldn't say so and you wouldn't show it!*

Yes!

J-M. *So . . . maybe you are an idiot too . . . AS WELL! But at least, if that is so, it seems to me that you assume it much more than you say it!*

(bursts out laughing) Thank you for the 'idiot'!

J-M. *I'm not saying that I myself think you're an idiot, but I'm saying that if YOU want to think of yourself as an idiot, you still seem to be quite comfortable with that, not making a drama out of it . . .*

Yes, that's true!

2-6

A Tee-shirt with a Bow Tie

I'm telling you about my dream. In a street that's still being built, I meet my first patient who comes up to me and asks for an appointment. He's a doctor, he looks like an administrator and is wearing a bow tie. I accept with some apprehension: an appointment is made for three o'clock the following afternoon. The next day, the place where we are meeting is still unfinished. I am wearing shorts and a tee-shirt and can't find anything more appropriate to wear. I eventually find a room where I can see my patient. I realize that I am very apprehensive about any legal or administrative questions my patient might ask me. The encounter takes place, but I have no memory of how it went.

J-M. *What is the atmosphere for you?*

Things being unfinished, construction, surprise. It's a beautiful bright day.

J-M. *Shall we look at some of the elements? Do you identify yourself with this unfinished office?*

Hmm . . . I'm an unfinished office . . . I'm looking . . . I am white, still unfinished, with areas of light and shadow. I am calm. I don't yet know what clothes I'll be wearing.

J-M. *Can you now 'be' the workmen who are busy finishing the work?*

I am wearing a safety helmet. I belong to a team that works well together. I know that the work is progressing. I am contributing to the building of the site. What I enjoy is being part of a work team. I am not alone.

J-M. *Can you 'be' the shorts and tee shirt?*

I am a white tee-shirt in motion, ready to be taken off. I am comfortable. I am leaving this comfort.

J-M. *Now, you are the tee shirt and you are speaking to the bow tie!*

I prefer to be in my shoes rather than yours, sir. I would rather be a loose and baggy tee-shirt than a bow tie.

J-M. *You are the bow tie and you are talking to the tee shirt. Do you receive what it says?*

I don't feel good. I like the amount of space you take up, sir — hey, I'm calling it "sir'! — It frightens me. You move a lot and I don't know where your center is.

J-M. *Tell it about yourself.*

I am reduced to rigidity. Part of me isn't alive. It's strangled. I feel myself shrinking.

J-M. *You have heard the bow tie. How do you receive it?*

As the tee-shirt or as Marie-Paule?

J-M. *As Marie Paule.*

What you say resonates with me and it must have belonged to me, and must still belong to me. I am reintegrating something that I recognize.

J-M. *You recognize that there is one Marie Paule who is very bow tie, and one who is very tee shirt and you told us you were getting ready to change. There are a lot of clothes here, as well as a safety helmet.*

My associations . . . uniform, that's something I hate! (her eyes fill with tears)

J-M. *What is this emotion you feel toward uniform?*

I can't stand it. I wore it for ten years. What can I wear to receive this patient?

J-M. *What you are evoking is a 'shorts and tee shirt' Marie Paule, a 'helmeted' Marie Paule, and a 'bow tied' Marie Paule, and now you want to change clothes but you don't know what to wear . . .*

Yes

J-M. *OK!* (getting up and taking her arm in his) *Let's go shopping!* (Laughter) *Look in shop windows* (the other participants in the room are implicitly representing the shops) *and choose something* (more laughter)

OK! Valériane's trousers, Monique's necklace, Ann's tee-shirt.

J-M. *Are you thinking in terms of changing, taking and throwing away? Your overall direction is right, but you need to learn how to direct it, is that right?*

Yes, my overall direction is fine. But changing clothes means I am looking for myself.

So what do the clothes you have chosen tell you about the next step you might make?

I've selected the trousers for their strict tailoring, the tee-shirt for harmony and the necklace for imagination.

J-M. *In terms of group dynamics, I am impressed that you have made a whole out of elements of two people who were in open conflict yesterday . . . (Laughter)*

Strictness and harmony. I am convinced that they (Valériane and Anne) are very close despite their differences. I'm reappropriating something that belongs to me.

Later comments from Marie-Paule

In my dream I notice a healer and a person who is healed, a therapist and a patient-therapist, represented by a tee-shirt and a bow tie respectively.

This work on my dream led me to become aware of a latent internal conflict between my creativity and my rigor. My rigor, represented by the bow tie and the managerial air of my doctor patient, is at the same time a hindrance (the constraint of the bow tie) and a possible recovery (being a doctor). I am afraid of rigor, whereas imagination reassures me: it is a mediating and moderating element which enables harmony to emerge. Imagination enables me to make a link between rigor and harmony, and to make both these elements exist. I notice that at the beginning of the dream these are not reconcilable. The fact of identifying with them, and making them meet and talk to each other made it possible for me to accommodate them, to initiate a reconciliation between them. At that time, I spontaneously made an association between them during this exercise with Jean-Marie. In a way I carried on the dream and found a solution to the conflict that was set up. A good demonstration of Perls's method.

The various situations that appear in the dream relate to the notions of ready/not ready (the fear of not being ready to practice, the office under construction), to relaxation/rigor (the tee-shirt and the bow tie), and doctor/patient (the healer and the healed). How do I construct myself within the space between these polarities?

I am aware of the importance of integrating the patient into my field, and accepting both rigor and harmony within my field. It is possible and necessary for these two elements to coexist. The tee-shirt symbolizes lightness and movement. The bow tie, heaviness and strangulation.

This lack of confidence in my own creativity is not something new, but it shows up with particular clarity in this dream. Spontaneous creativity was crushed by parental prohibitions, and it was that process that made me afraid of rigor and frameworks.

My dream uses my professional situation to bring to light this difficulty which predates it by a long time, the antagonism between creativity and rigor. In 'real life' I am facing having to find a way from an unbearable work situation, where the individual, wearing both a literal and metaphorical uniform, is denied in the interests of team work, to a future as a therapist whose work consists precisely of helping the autonomy and richness of the patient's psyche to emerge . . .

What is the role of creativity in the world of work? The tee-shirt, for me, is movement, liberty, space. The bow tie to me is not just strangulation but everything rigid, serious and conventional. During my childhood my mother both personified and imposed rigor and seriousness, whereas my father possessed imagination and creativity although repressed. In contact with each of them, nothing of that kind could be expressed so I often hid any possibility of creativeness. The rigidity of one and the depression of the other increased at the same rate in parallel, and were equally destructive. After a depressive episode my father finally allowed his creative inspiration to emerge and began working with wood and making fine furniture.

So creativity did appear within the family circle, as manifested by my father. But a stifling rigor never let go its grip on my mother. This situation resulted in an overt conflict, a context which was hardly conducive to children flourishing . . . It was much easier for me to get in touch with my creativity outside the family environment, by 'escaping' physically or mentally: the field of possibilities was then open, and I was able to access my creativity.

By helping me in this work, Jean-Marie enabled me to get back into the movement of creation. I have really been able to appreciate the importance of the therapist's involvement, and the importance of joint creation. Jean-Marie's suggestion to me to 'go shopping,' by choosing clothes worn by members of the group, enabled me, by accessing my ego-function, to reach a very peaceful kind of reintegration. From then on, the clothes selected themselves.

It is strange to note that this internalized antagonism has emerged in an almost deliberately recreated form in my professional life . . . Working on the dream, getting in touch with the emotion that uniform created in me made it possible to access this whole hidden aspect of my life. By becoming consciously aware of this whole dynamic I have finally been able to begin the work of disengaging from my parents' conflict, to start regaining my inner wholeness and finding my own autonomy once more.

Note:
This dream and the also the next one, and the commentaries which follow, are extracts from an article written by a group of students who took part in a workshop on dreams in Gestalt therapy led by the author. Reading the article will help the reader understand better the kind of approach adopted here. Caudron, S., et al. "Deux approches du rêve en Gestalt-thérapie" ("Two approaches to dreams in Gestalt therapy") in *Cahiers de Gestalt thérapie* no. 10, Automne 2001, pp. 29-55.

2-7

THE MAN, DANGER AND SALVATION

J-M. *Is it a recent dream?*

It's from last night. I had two! I saw myself on the steps of my grandmother's big house and my friend's son was there and he was shaving my legs. It was rather erotic. Then, I was inside, near the kitchen table, there was a black curtain, a body all in black stretched out face down. There was sticky stuff on the floor. It was dirty. The body dressed in black got up slowly, it was a stranger, he had a beard and I was afraid. My friend was downstairs, but I couldn't call him, I just let out a little cry and I was able to open the door. The man in black disappeared. I don't like dreams where I have to cry out, yet I can't. I feel a conflict between inertia and the desire to move.

J-M. *Do you think the elements of your dream are connected?*

There was some danger that I imagined: the danger came from the man, but salvation came from the man too.

J-M. *I feel addressed here; there is some kind of parallelism. Is this the first time that you have sat down there for a 'demonstration' with me in front of the group? How have I managed to make you so afraid up till now, but now begin to speak out?*

I feel hot. (She takes her jacket off)

J-M. *You are taking off your black jacket.*

Ah! (laughs) Yes, it seems as if the danger comes from men.

J-M. *I'm not referring to MEN in general. I'm referring to myself.*

(Silence) Yes, but the fact that you are a man counts for a lot. The first time, when I met you, I didn't find you frightening, and I even found that you left me a good deal of space.

I felt very small in front of you, who are so big, and also that was happening in the group, where there were no landmarks, and I felt lost. I find you very intelligent and I was afraid of not coming up to your level.

J-M. *(I listen, I support her with my gaze)*

There was a certain severity, something uncompromising, and I did not appreciate it.
It was like when you suggested guiding me through a drawing that we did in the first session. I couldn't handle standing in

front of you. I might as well have been flat on my face, even speechless.

J-M. *It's not clear . . . , how do I go about making you afraid? Obviously for you to feel that you're not up to it suggests some kind of humiliation but I can't see where the fear comes in. How do you hang your fear on that experience?*

I don't know.

J-M. *I see that you have almost stopped breathing.*

I can't see what I might be risking. There is my relationship with men in general.

J-M. *How could I be someone who might shave your legs and how could that become erotic?*

(She laughs)

J-M. *What did you understand?*

Just you, shaving me. (In a 'little girl' voice)

J-M. *And is this the aspect that you would be interested in understanding?*

Yes.

J-M. *Might you be afraid of me shaving you, symbolically speaking, and of finding it erotic?*

I think I might find it frightening and at the same time I might want it. Why not?
But with the feeling of leaping into a precipice, losing all my bearings, not being myself anymore, being nothing.

J-M. *You seem to be talking about suicide here!*

But knowing that I wasn't going to die. It's as if I liked these kinds of losing myself, not knowing who I am anymore.

J-M. *Might you be telling me: "In my relationship with you, Jean Marie, I can run the risk of losing myself, because I know that I won't lose myself completely?"*

Yes, that's it. (Silence)

J-M. *What are you feeling now?*

I'm thinking about seduction and . . . (Silence)
It's as if you weren't a figure of seduction for me, not physically. I don't get the idea that you intend to seduce, and that's something new for me. Also the fact that I trusted you sufficiently to have come here.
(Long silence)

J-M. *Are you cutting off?*

I don't know what I'm talking about. I can't understand why I was afraid of you, I don't think I'm afraid any more. In fact, I'm not sure that I was frightened of you. Not like Denis (a member of the group), who is somebody I am frightened of! Denis has a beard too!

J-M. *In your dream, it's more the fear of being silenced than fear of being frightened. Perhaps I was transmitting that your silence with me was due to fear. The bearded man who frightens you in your dream! Perhaps I should get myself a shave?!!!*

Is it the masculinity of the beard? Yes, it's a sign of manhood for me. I am very attracted to that but it frightens me. And the fact that I'm unable to cry out, I've dreamed that dozens of times.

J M. In this dream, the man may be both danger and salvation.

He's the only source of security, even, without the man I'm nothing. It's only him who endangers me and saves me.

J-M. *This double movement . . . , how could you maintain a dis tanced relationship with me, and how can you, now, feel safe. And the third man, who is a child but yet erotic, or erotic and yet a child?*

Yes! At the point when it started to get erotic, he wasn't a little boy any more. That's very worrying!

J-M. *Am I wrong or do I get the impression that there are moments of to ing and fro ing here?*

Yes, it swings backward and forward.

J-M. *Does that mean any thing to you, does it say anything to you?*

The idea of being attracted and going away.

J-M. *Can you try saying it to me? For example, "Jean Marie, you attract me and you frighten me, I'm withdrawing!"*

It's difficult.

J-M. *Too difficult?!*

I want to go forward but all I do is withdraw . . . When I say that, I don't feel anything particular for you.

J-M. *What do I do to make you feel that way?*

I feel alone.

J-M. *Strange, because you're saying it to ME.*

I'm trying. I don't know.

J-M. *You're withdrawing!*

Yes.

J-M. *Are you sure? What are you telling me with that smile?*

I'm on the edge of the precipice but I don't know.

J-M. *Would you like to go further or not?*

I can't see very far ahead.

J-M. *Is that: I can't, or I won't?*

It's already very far away. What stays with me is the ambivalent image of the man who is capable of having so much power over me, the one I'm afraid of.

J-M. *There's no ambivalence there then.*

No, but it's often the man I'm most afraid of who will be able to console me!

I'm thinking about my father here! Who can make me withdraw and who can't make me go further, or save me.

J-M. *Do you want to carry on?*

No, that's OK.

Eliane's comments

When I put myself forward to work with Jean-Marie, I was afraid and did not feel safe. I had a fear of men and fear of my own words. Merely retelling it now plunges me into the same emotional state, my heart is beating fast and I find it difficult to breathe.

At the beginning of the interview I felt myself existing and felt supported by the gentleness of his voice, as if he put forms into it. I felt that he was not there to break me and I was able to have sufficient confidence in him. Also, during the work I found that he maintained a certain distance from me. His gaze was always present. It was like a light for me. I felt that I was respected and accompanied wherever I was, as if he knew what I needed.

On several occasions Jean-Marie's interventions surprised me, as when he said: "How have I managed to make you so afraid up till now, and now you start to speak out?" These surprise effects got me moving, I find that being surprised is very exciting and it makes everything come alive. Also, I was confident enough to be surprised and yet not keep silent.

What stays with me from the dream, is "How have I managed to shut your mouth?" Since I've done this work, a space has opened up and I realize that a lot of people, in my life, shut my mouth. And I ask myself: "How do I manage to let so many people shut my mouth?", it's something that's still active now. And yet I'm a talkative person!

I was also surprised when Jean-Marie suggested "shaving me." At that moment, it was as if I was launching out into the void, some part of me couldn't be there, and I was so anxious I cut off. It seems suicidal, but what was retreating was very alive but not active. And I realized as I said it that it was a refusal of contact. Except that on this occasion I stayed there, and by allowing me to speak, he made me exist, my words were embodied. I was aware of moments when I was there or not there.

What has also changed is that now I am less afraid of my friend, who used to put me in a blue funk, to such a point that I couldn't move.

See note at end of previous chapter.

CONCLUSION

BETWEEN THEORY AND PRACTICE

Practice is grounded in theory but there is a gap. Theory is grounded in practice but there is a distance. Practice demonstrates theory, implicitly and explicitly, and theory is an attempt to give form to experience lived in practice. And something always escapes through the crack between them. And we search, and I search, endlessly, to shrink this gap because of my need for greater coherence, no doubt deriving from some vestigial fantasy of omnipotence. But this irreducible lack of coherence also gives rise to movement. Perfect coherence is closure, the end of a process, the finished *gestaltung*, death.

And yet . . . "The form exists the ground" as Maldiney wrote.

Reflexivity

The concept of "self" which is the theoretical foundation of Gestalt therapy cannot be translated into French, despite the efforts of some French authors and editors to promote its translation as "*soi*." Scholars of the English language who have studied this little word have shown that its use as a noun — "the" self — is relatively recent. Many believe it to be the result of philosophers or psychologists reifying something which everyday language treats in a far more dynamic way: *self* is used primarily as a prefix or suffix, that is, as an auxiliary with a reflexive function. "Self-control" and "self-service" are some of the terms that French has imported from English to refer to a concept only available to those of us writing in French through long-winded paraphrase. In a self-service facility, I act — I perform some service — and I am also the recipient of this service. The "I" who serves and the "I" who receives are of course one and the same and are joined in the single word "self," whereas French would have "je me sers" (literally, "I serve me") thereby marking a distinction between the "I" and the "me." This is what we traditionally refer to as self-reflexivity, the mirroring process through which my acting on the world simultaneously acts to define myself.

It is easy to understand how this operation of "self-something" or "something-self" leads to the resulting entity of THE self, and to the permanent oscillation between an I-as-process and an I-as-entity found among philosophers, psychologists and others, including the founders of Gestalt therapy.

But what English ratifies in this way is the experience whereby the self, through acting, through contact, both acts AND constructs itself from minute to minute. It is noteworthy that when I attempted above to render the idea of "self-service" in French I was impelled to write "I serve myself," that is, using a verb in order to denote an action.

So one of my frequent working methods involves giving concrete form to self-reflexivity. It would be inappropriate here to cite the many works which have emphasized the real and symbolic importance of the mirror in human development. From Lacan to Kohut, from Piaget to Dolto, the reflection in the mirror plays a key role in identity formation, just as it may also lead to inflections that may be termed pathological, as the story of Narcissus shows.

Carl Rogers made the reflecting intervention one of the cornerstones of his approach: reflection is a word that acts as a visual metaphor. We could also, moving into the realm of auditory metaphor, speak of an echo, or resonance, or of reverberation as Bachelard recommended.

This mirroring, through words and sometimes gesture, of what I see and hear of the other is essential to his or her formation. The other tells me or shows me who I am. The child who breaks a glass and is told "You're stupid" perceives a reflection of what s/he demonstrated, even unintentionally, with this act, and this reflection is formative. The "self breaks" the glass, if I may put it like this, and "someone" reflects back the act by signaling that it is a "stupid self." The therapist's possible silence is also a form of reflection and should not, as so often, be confused with neutrality.

Just as the mirror image is merely a partial reflection of "reality," if only because it is reversed and two — rather than three — dimensional, what the therapist reflects back is a curtailed, selected and distorted experience. Rogers, for example, used the reflection principally to illustrate the concealed affect in the patient's words. Whatever kind of reflection the therapist provides, it will stress one aspect of experience over another, and this is unavoidable. Hence it may have a clarifying or structuring function, a provocative or supportive function, it may generate confusion or emotion, produce meaning or decentering, and so on. The choice of what the therapist selects as the figure will no doubt reflect both his or her own sensibility and theoretical reference system. But I am concerned here not with the contents or the forms of this reverberation but the crucial role they play in attaining the goal of continuing individuation, that is, the process of the self in motion. In the absence of any novel feedback, human beings will often remain attached to a fixed representation of previous echoes; even when they attempt something new or try to activate creative contacts they will find it difficult to construct new representations if the situation, or the other person within that situation, fails to reflect any novelty to them.

Experience Is Contact

Where other therapeutic approaches posit the psyche as the fundamental paradigm, Gestalt therapy posits contact. All human experience is first and foremost contact with the world, and the psyche is only a crystallized and secondary form of this. Contact is the primary experience. The therapist's patients, however, are more prone to see their suffering as located in the psyche than in contact. And they use the contact that occurs to confirm their own "psychic contents." Hence it is through placing different kinds of contact at the center of therapeutic work that experience can take on new meanings. Whereas the patient thinks things over in isolation, I think in terms of interacting and relating within the situation. If the patient is afraid, we will seek together to discover why the environment may seem — or may have seemed — menacing. If the patient complains of feeling too small, we can begin to explore the question of "smaller than whom?," or the humiliations they experienced as a result of their small stature. Human beings *are* contact. Gestalt therapy has developed the concept of "contact boundary" to refer to experience. Thinking in terms of contact boundary is probably the major difficulty for those new to the theory and practice of Gestalt therapy since it breaks with centuries of "psychic" tradition. By way of explanation I sometimes use the following example. In the usual course of events, I am not conscious of my hand existing and I feel no particular sensation in it. If I place my hand on an object or a person, this act makes me feel both my hand and the object. Touching this object makes it real to my sense of touch and similarly this touch gives feeling and hence existence to my hand. It is the operation of contact itself which gives existence to the other and to me and at the same time marks our difference. The same operation both separates and joins. In the absence of contact there is no differentiation, and in the absence of differentiation there is no contact and hence no experience. Touch only exists if it is the touch *of* something; sight is neither the eye alone nor the object alone but the oval of vision. Similarly, Husserl stated that consciousness *as such* did not "exist," and that there was only consciousness OF something, even when consciousness is directed at itself.

This method constitutes a radical delocalization of human experience, and so dichotomies such as interior/exterior or superficial/deep lose their relevance and meaning. This method of receiving and listening reframes the patient's experience and sheds a new light on it, thereby introducing the possibility of movement, since any shift involves movement.

Acting in the Middle Mode

Our founders saw the middle mode as one of the self's characteristics. In developing their theory of the self in a situation of creative adjustment they drew upon two paradigmatic situations: the child playing and the artist creating. The theory of the creative act owes much to Otto Rank (of whose *Art and the Artist* Perls, Hefferline, & Goodman wrote " . . . is beyond praise").

What they say about the child at play seems to draw heavily on the work of George Herbert Mead, although they do not cite his influence. Mead's *Mind, Self and Society*, published in 1934, opened up the concept of the self, and drew a large part of its argument from the study of children at play.

The middle mode, or middle voice, is a concept borrowed from the grammar of Ancient Greek. In the case of directly reflexive action, Ancient Greek used the middle mode, whereas we use a reflexive pronoun such as 'me.' The middle mode indicates that the subject is personally involved in the action he or she undertakes, that he/her self (active) is acting for or on behalf of him/her self (beneficiary, passive).

The creative artist engages body and soul with action. The painter works on the canvas in an active way and the colors placed on the canvas give rise to perceptions and sensations which in turn constantly influence the act of creation. The same process occurs with the child at play.

In this concept of the middle mode through which the founding theorists refined their concept of the self we can see once more the crucial concept of the self which I discussed above in the context of reflexivity.

It may be appropriate to relate this to the concept of "free-floating attention" which psychoanalysts use to refer to the way in which they listen. We can glimpse here in embryonic form the genesis of the middle mode, of the "to and fro" presence, if I may call it that. But the middle mode which defines the self in Gestalt therapy is not limited to attention. It is global in scope, integrated and integrative of different modes of experience, the sensory, the motor, and the affective and so on.

Spontaneity

The second basic characteristic of the self is spontaneity. The spontaneity Perls and Goodman recommend is very close to the middle mode. They often see it as in a dialogue with deliberateness though they sometimes oppose it. Certainly therapeutic work, with its slowing down of actions and words in order to widen the field of awareness, may seem to privilege deliberateness at the cost of spontaneity. This might be an egotistic "experimental neurosis" produced by the therapeutic situation which will ultimately have to be dissolved in order to bring about integration with a rediscovered creativity. In this respect, the therapist's spontaneity should not be seen as some kind of impulsivity or reactivity. The spontaneous reactions of a pilot flying an Airbus in a tricky situation are quite unlike those I would have if placed in the same situation! The spontaneous improvisation of the jazz pianist hardly produces the same results as the improvisation of a five-year-old discovering a piano keyboard. Moreno used to define spontaneity as the capacity to respond appropriately to a new situation, or to produce a new response to a common situation. The psychotherapist's spontaneity enables her to show support for the patient by putting her hand on the patient's shoulder, by joking with him, by revealing certain of her emotional reactions . . . but it can never be justified solely by reference to her own feelings. The therapist's spontaneity is one aspect of the atmospherics of the situation, all the more so if the patient has been obliged to exercise a close control over entire areas of his existence which has contributed to the emergence of his pathology.

Engaged with the Situation

It is the psychotherapist's immediate experience of the situation which enables him to engage with it. Even though he may have to bracket off his own system of values and references, the Gestalt psychotherapist is engaged in the encounter and involved in co-creating the gestalt of that moment jointly with the patient he is accompanying. His presence cannot be seen as neutral because he is there face to face with the patient and enters into her field of experience. Paradoxical as it may seem, this engagement is rooted in the fundamental uncertainty which is a feature of the therapist's presence. The therapist is constantly required to *no longer* know and to not cling to acquired knowledge in order to make the patient's experience fit with it, like Procrustes' bed. Otto Rank claimed that every patient forces us to rethink the whole of psychopathology.

Although it is relatively easy to "get involved" everyone will have soon realized that the difficult part is maintaining that involvement. It is this sustained involvement which is one of the major functions of psychotherapy.

Holding On

Holding on, containing, supporting, retaining, detaining . . . A number of these tasks have already been subject to commentary by psychotherapists of all persuasions. Here I will limit myself to consideration of holding on, almost in the sense of "hanging on." During figure-construction, particularly in the initial stage of fore-contact, there are many opportunities for dilution, collapse, interruption, avoidance, premature solution of dilemmas and hasty selection of materials presented in the interests of using what is familiar. The quality of the current moment and its uniqueness given the new parameters of the situation may be lost if systems of representation linked to previous experience intervene prematurely. The unknown is interpreted in relation to the known, and novelty may be seen but not noticed. *Chronos* crushes *Kairos*:* chronology reasserts itself and the moment's ephemeral events go unremarked. What is novel is replaced by an archive.

From the very first words uttered in a meeting, a figure begins to take form. Certainly this form is vague at first, but its contours cry out to be shaped, and dialogue, both explicit and implicit, helps them emerge. Each consequent step refines the previous one, as long as the listener recognizes this. It is the therapist's role to choose to "listen" to each word, each phrase, each utterance, as the "logical" follow-up to what went before . . . or to decide to hear it as resistance, diversion or avoidance. Again, it is a question of holding on, of maintaining the tension and of supporting this process of going-towards an unknown which cannot yet be put into words but whose form emerges through fumbling attempts and sketchy outlines and which can only fully appear and unfold within and through the encounter.

Involvement

For me, getting involved means placing myself within the folds of the other's experience. IN-volvement. If I do not

---

* The ancient Greeks had two words for time, *Chronos,* referring to ordered sequential time, and *Kairos,* meaning an unspecified time when some important change may occur, a moment of opportunity. [Translator's note]

become involved, my EX-planations will be based on EX-ternalities. Too often psychotherapists who claim to be involved are only explaining themselves, putting their inner folds on view to the other.

There is constant debate within the profession about how far a psychotherapist's involvement and self-revelation should extend, which may give rise to uncertainty during supervision. People's ethics in such cases cannot be just a set of simplified and often de-contextualized rules. However, some questions and observations may be able to help practitioners to clarify their own practice.

The first question that arises is almost a truism: who benefits from the therapist's involvement? It is tempting to reply that of course it benefits the patient. But is it that simple? How can this involvement be purged of narcissistic, egocentric, tranquilizing and other elements deriving from the therapist, let alone any perverse or hysterical components?

One criterion for evaluating this involvement seems to lie in its relation to the figure that the patient is busy constructing. Of course, the "relevance principle" of Lewin's work on the field stipulates that any event (and the emergence of a thought, a memory or an association *is* an event for the therapist) should not *a priori be* separated from the situation as irrelevant. But the fact that it is linked with the present moment is not necessarily a justification for expressing it! What I would warn against is the danger of de-centering the patient's own experience in favor of the therapist's experience. In such situations, involvement may support avoidance rather than supporting the work in progress.

It has seldom been my experience, whether as patient, psychotherapist or supervisor, that long accounts of a psychotherapist's own lived experience are of any great interest. I am not denying that a patient might feel supported by a demonstration of fellow-feeling, but I am afraid of the possible covering that might follow. Of course I also fear that this kind of disguised interpretation and transmission of meaning may pass on a model.

But I insist on the distinction between this narrative voice and the emerging "voice" of the situation. With reference to my discussion of "intentionality," I would argue that the systematic, moment-by-moment study of the way in which I am affected by the situation and the joint work we are undertaking, or by what I perceive as coming from the patient, is essential for detecting emergent aims and intentions in search of what comes next. To use Merleau-Ponty's terms once more, the therapist's expressions of involvement may then truly become "speaking words," that is, speech that seeks to become meaningful while uttering — or stuttering — the present. In such moments, I mumble about the experience of the moment. I speak as best I can. "It" speaks as best "it" can! This kind of speech differs from what Merleau-Ponty calls "spoken speech" which is grounded in acquired meanings and "rejoices in the meanings available as in newly-acquired riches." This spoken speech is that of the psychotherapist speaking him or herself, relating lived experience and systems of representation and opening up his or her "archives," to use a favorite term of Foucault's.

What Follows Next: a Thinking Presence Oriented to Possibilities

Our way of thinking during a session often owes much to our habit of understanding or explaining any present situation as a function of what happened yesterday or previously, during the person's past history. I would like to share here a very ancient Taoist fable which also illustrates a change of paradigm.

> *This Chinese story concerns a farmer who lived in a poor village in the country. He was considered lucky because he had a horse that he used when working in the fields or traveling. One day, his horse ran away. All his neighbors commiserated with him for his misfortune, but the farmer merely said: "Maybe!"*
>
> *A few days later, the horse came back, bringing with him two wild horses. The villagers rejoiced at his good fortune, but the farmer simply said "Maybe!"*
>
> *The next day, the farmer's son tried to mount one of the wild horses: the horse threw him and he broke a leg. The neighbors expressed their sympathy for this misfortune, but the farmer said only "Maybe!"*

> *The following week, recruiting officers came to the village to pres gang the young men into the army because of the war. They rejected the farmer's son because of his broken leg. When the neighbors told him how lucky he was, the farmer replied "Maybe!"*

Of all possible meanings we can read into this tale I should like to emphasize just one: the meaning of an experience is established by what follows it, not by what came before. Of course we could discuss it endlessly and discover a multitude of reasons why the horse ran away: the paddock fence was not strong enough, the farmer had not kept an eye on him because . . . or because . . . But the story shows just how the future bestows meaning, to the point where any desire to refer back the past is quenched through lack of interest. Is this one possible direction for psychotherapy?

One dominant epistemological tradition sees any attribution of meaning to history as dependent on what precedes an event, in a more or less linear chain of causation. This approach is now considered almost scientific, and has a near monopoly of "meaning." Even if its scientific basis is questionable, it is seen as the clinical diagnostic attitude par excellence. Sometimes this clinical attitude may be confused with a psychotherapeutic approach. However I prefer to argue that the clinical attitude and the psychotherapeutic attitude derive from two very dissimilar approaches. Anyone who needs to be convinced of this has merely to open any work of clinical psychology or psychopathology where they will find detailed descriptions of patients, their behaviors and their symptoms, their affects and their environment, with no questioning of the way in which such knowledge is acquired. The observer or the clinician rarely makes an appearance and, more often than not, the patient is reified by the gaze of experts who habitually deny the conditions under which they encounter the patient. Again, this is still the method used in one-person psychology, but we are justified in questioning its relevance to a form of psychotherapy which is based almost entirely on the encounter.

So these different forms of psychotherapy should develop on the basis of dyadic, two-person, psychology. It is most likely not science — or scientism — which will usher in such developments, in the absence of a change of orientation that might force it to confront its ideological blindness. In the current state of affairs it is most probably philosophy and certain sociological and epistemological approaches which will provide the most useful tools for going beyond an exclusive reliance on clinical psychology and psychopathology toward understanding the psychotherapeutic encounter as an experience, a mutative, a transformative experience since transformation can only operate "on the occasion of an other."

BIBLIOGRAPHY

Barwise, Jon. 1989. *The situation in logic, CSLI lecture notes*. Stanford, CA: Center for the Study of Language and Information.

Benasayag, M. 1998. *Le mythe de l'individu*. Paris: Coll. Armillaire, La Découverte.

Berger, P., Luckmann, T. 1966. *La construction sociale de la réalité*. 2nd ed. Paris: Méridiens Klinksleck.

Binswanger, L. 1970. Apprendre par expérience, comprendre, interpréter en psychanalyse. In *Discours Parcours et Freud*: Gallimard. Original edition, 1955.

Blankenburg, W. 1991. La signification de la phénoménologie pour la psychothérapie. In *Psychiatrie et Existence*, edited by Fedida, P., et al. Millon: Coll. Krisis.

Boss, M. 1959. *Introduction à la médecine psychosomatique*. trad. de l'allemand par Georgi W. Paris: PUF. Original edition, 1954.

Braque, G. 1994. *Cahier*. Paris: Editions Maeght. Original edition, 1917-1955.

Brentano, F. 1944. *Psychologie du point de vue empirique*. Paris: Aubier. Original edition, 1874.

Cavaleri, P. 1992. Le concept d'intentionnalité en phénoménologie et en Gestalt-thérapie, traduit de l'italien. *Documents de l'IFGT* 56.

Chemouni, J., ed. 2001. *Clinique de l'intentionnalité*. Paris: Éditions In Press.

Combes, M. 1999. *Simondon   Individu et collectivité*. Philosophies. Paris: PUF.

Dastur, F. 1992. Phénoménologie et thérapie: La question de l'autre dans les Zollikoner Seminäre. In *Figures de la subjectivité*, edited by Courtine, J. F. Paris: Editions du C.N.R.S.

De Montaigne, M. 1603. *The essayes*. Translated by Florio, J. London: V. Sims.

Debord, G. 2000. *Rapport sur la construction des situations suivi de Les situationnistes et les nouvelles formes d'action dans la poli*. Paris: Éditions Mille et une Nuits.

Deleuze, G. 1968. *Différence et répétition*. Paris: PUF.

———. 1969. *Logique du sens*. Paris: Les éditions de Minuit

Dewey, J. 1993. *Art as experience*. New York: Capricorn Books. Original edition, 1934.

———. 1993. *Logique, la théorie de l'enquête,*. Paris: PUF. Original edition, 1938.

Dorra, M. 2001. *Heidegger, Primo Levi et le séquoia*. Paris: Traces-Gallimard.

Dubet, F. 1994. *Sociologie de l'expérience*. Paris: Seuil.

Epstein, E. K. 1995. The narrative turn: postmodern theory and systemic therapy. *Gestalt Theory* 17 (3).

Fédida, P., Schotte J., ed. 1991. *Psychiatrie et existence, Décade de Cerisy*. Grenoble: Jerome Millon.

Fink, E. 1952. L'analyse intentionnelle et le problème de la pensée spéculative. In *Problèmes actuels de la phènomèno logie. Textes de P. Thèvenaz [and others]*, edited by van Breda, H. L. Paris: Bruges.

Fornel, Michel De, and Quéré, Louis. 1999. *La logique des situa tions: nouveaux regards sur l'écologie des activités sociales*. Raisons pratiques, Paris: Editions de l'Ecole des Hautes Etudes en Sciences Sociales.

Freud, S. 1937. Konstruktionen in der analyse. *Internationale Zeitschrift für Psychoanalyse* 23 (4).

———. 1991. *Le moi et le ça, Oeuvres complètes*. Paris: PUF. Original edition, 1921-1923.

Gergen, K. J. 1992. *The saturated self.* New York: Basic Books.

———. 1994. *Realities and relationships*. Cambridge: Harvard University Press.

Gibson, J.J. 1979. *The ecological approach to visual perception*. Boston: Houghton Mifflin.

Goffman, E. & Winkin, Y. 1988. *Les Moments et leurs hommes*. Paris: Seuil Minuit.

Goodman, Paul. 1972. *Little prayers and finite experience,*. New York: Harper & Row.

———. 1994. *Crazy hope and finite experience: Final essays of Paul Goodman (Edited by Taylor Stoehr)*. San Francisco: Jossey-Bass. Original edition, New York: Harper & Row, 1972.

Gordon, P. 1999. *Face to face*. Constable: London.

Groddeck, G. 1973. *Le livre du ça.* Paris: Gallimard. Original edition, 1923.

Heidegger, M. 1962. *Being and time.* New York: Harper & Row.

———. 1976. *Acheminement vers la parole.* Paris: Classiques de la Philosophie. Original edition, 1959, Paris, NRF-Gallimard.

———. 1992. Zollikoner Seminare, Klostermann. Cité par Dastur F., Phénoménologie et thérapie : la question de l'autre dans les zollikoner Seminare. In *Figures de la subjectivité*, edited by Courtine, J. F. Parid: Editions du CNRS. Original edition, 1987.

———. 2001. *Zollikon Seminars, Protocols, Conversations, Letters.* Edited by Boss, M. Evanston IL: Northwestern University Press. Original edition, 1987.

Husserl, E. 1950. *Idées directrices pour une phénoménologie, Tome 1.* Paris: Gallimard. Original edition, 1913.

Joas, H. 1999. *La créativité de l'agir.* Translated by Rusch, P. Paris: Ed. du Cerf. Original edition, 1992.

Kaufmann, P. 1968. *Kurt Lewin, Une théorie du champ dans les Sciences de l'Homme.* Paris: Vrin.

Kimbura, B. 1992. *Réflexion et quête du soi, Ecrits de psychopathologie phénoménologique.* Paris: PUF-Psychiatrie ouverte.

King, L., ed. 1999. *Committed uncertainty in psychotherapy Essays in honour of Peter Lomas.* London: Whurr Publishers.

Latner, J. 1983. This is the speed of light. *The Gestalt Journal* VI (2).

Lévinas, E. 1974. Intentionnalité et sensation. In *En découvrant l'existence avec Husserl et Heidegger*. Paris: Vrin. Original edition, 1974.

———. 1990. *Nine Talmudic readings*. Translated by Aronowicz, A. Bloomington, Ind.: Indiana University Press. Original edition, 1968.

———. 1998. *Discovering existence with Husserl and Heidegger*. Evanston IL: Northwestern University Press. Original edition, 1965. *En découvrant l'existence avec Husserl et Heidegger*. Paris: Vrin.

Lévinas, E. & Nemo, Philippe. 1982. *Ethique et infini*. Paris: Fayard/Livre de Poche Biblio-Essais.

Lewin, K. 1935. *Dynamic theory of personality*. New York: McGraw-Hill.

———. 1938. *Resolving social conflicts*. Washington DC: American Psychological Association.

———. 1952. *Field theory in social science*. London: Travistock Publications.

———. 1959. *Psychologie dynamique*. 4th ed. Paris: PUF. Original edition, 1969.

Lyotard, J. F. 1979. *La condition post moderne*. Paris: Les éditions de Minuit.

Maldiney, H. 1973. *Regard parole espace*. Lausanne: Amers - L' âge d'Homme.

Maldiney, H. 1991. *Penser l'homme et la folie: A la lumiére de l'analyse existentielle et de l'analyse du destin, Collection Krisis*. Grenoble: J. Millon.

Maldiney, H. 1991. Vers quelle phénoménologie de l'art. *Art et Phénoménologie 7*.

———. 1994. Esquisse d'une phénoménologie de l'Art. In *L'art au regard de la phénoménologie, Colloque de l'Ecole des Beaux Arts de Toulouse*. Toulouse: Presses Univ. du Mirail.

Marrow, A. J. 1972. *Kurt Lewin, sa vie, son oeuvre*. Paris: ESF. Original edition, 1969.

Maslow, A. 1962. *Towards a psychology of being*. Princeton NJ: Van Nostrand.

Mcleod, L. 1995. The self in Gestalt therapy theory. *British Gestalt Journal* 2 (1).

Mcnamee, S., Gergen, J. K. 1992. *Therapy as social construction*. London: Sage.

Merleau-Ponty, M. 1945. *Phénoménologie de la perception*. Paris: Gallimard.

———. 1964. *Le visible et l'invisible*. Paris: Gallimard.

Michaux, H. 1972. *La vie dans les plis*. Paris: NRF-Gallimard.

Miller, M.V. 2001. *La poétique de la Gestalt thérapie*. Bordeaux: L'exprimerie.

Minkowski, E. 1999. *Traité de psychopathologie*. Les empêcheurs de penser en rond. Le Plessis-Robinson: Institut Synthé labo. Original edition, Paris: Presses universitaires de France, 1966.

Novalis. 2002. *Le monde doit être romantisé*. Translated by Schefer, O. Paris: Éditions Allia. Original edition, 1798.

Parlett, M. 1991. Reflections on field theory. *British Gestalt Journal* 1 (2).

———. 1993. Towards a more Lewinian Gestalt therapy. *British Gestalt Journal* 2 (2).

Perls, F. 1968. *Gestalt therapy verbatim*. Walnut Creek, CA: Real People Press.

Perls, F., Hefferline, R. & Goodman, P. 1994. *Gestalt therapy: Excitement and growth in the human personality*. Gouldsboro, ME: The Gestalt Journal Press. Original edition, New York: Julian Press, 1951.

———. 2001. *Gestalt thérapie*. Bordeaux: L'exprimerie. Original edition, New York: Julian Press, 1951.

Pessoa, F. L. 1988. *Le livre de l'intranquillité*. Vol. 1, *Oeuvres de Fernando Pessoa*. Paris: C. Bourgois.

Polster, E. 1987. *Every person's life is worth a novel*. Gouldsboro, ME: The Gestalt Journal Press. Original edition, 1987 New York: W.W. Norton.

Ponge, F. 1971. *La fabrique du Pré*. Paris: Les sentiers de la création, Skira.

Pontalis, J.-B. 1975. *Trouver, accueillir, reconnaître l'absent*. Paris: Gallimard.

———. 1977. *Entre le rêve et la douleur*. Paris: Gallimard.

Prinzhorn, H. 1984. Expressions de la folie: Trad. Franç. Gallimard.

Queysanne, B. & Maldiney, H. 1985. *Philosophie Et De L'Architecture; La Fondation Maeght a St Paul De Vence*. Grenoble: Ecole D'Architecture De Grenoble.

Rank, O. 1985. *L'art et l'artiste*. Paris: Payot. Original edition, New York: A. A. Knopf, 1932.

Ricoeur, P. 1990. *Soi même comme un autre*. Paris: Seuil.

Robine, J. 1973. Expression, liberté d'impressions. *Thérapie Psychomotrice* 43.

———. 1991. Contact, the first experience. *The Gestalt Journal* XIV (1).

———. 1992. Un album d'entretiens à propos de Paul Goodman. *Revue Gestalt* 3.

———. 1996. The unknown carried into relationships. *British Gestalt Journal* 12 (3).

———. 1997. Is there a common ground on which we can build? *The Gestalt Journal* XX (2).

———. 1997. *Pli et dépli du self*. Bordeaux: Presses de l'IFGT.

———. 1998. *Gestalt thérapie, la construction du soi*. Paris: L'Harmattan.

———. 2001. From field to situation. In *Contact and relation ship in a field perspective*, edited by Robine, J. Bordeaux: Editions L'Exprimerie.

———. ed. 2006. *La psychotherapie comme esthétique*. Bordeau: Editions L'exprimerie.

Robine, J.-M., & Lapeyronnie, B. 1997. La confluence, expérience liée et experience aliénée. In *Gestalt thérapie, la construction du soi*, edited by Robine, J. Paris: L'Harmattan.

Rosset, C. 1999. *Loin de moi*. Paris: Editions de Minuit.

Roussillon, R. 1992. Voyager dans le temps. *Revue Française de Psychanalyse* LVI.

Rowan, J. 1990. *Subpersonalities: The people inside us*. London: Routledge.

Sartre, J-P. 1956. *Being and nothingness; an essay on pheno menological ontology*. New York: Philosophical Library. Original edition, 1949, Paris, Gallimard (L'être et le néant).

Searle, J.R. 1985. *L'intentionnalité. Essai de philosophie des états mentaux*. Paris: Editions de Minuit. Original edition, 1983.

Simondon, G. 1995. *L'individu et sa genèse physico biologique (l'individuation à la lumière des notions de forme et d'information)* Paris: CUF. Original edition, 1964.

Staemmler, F. 1997. Cultivating uncertainty : An attitude for Gestalt therapists. *British Gestalt Journal* 6 (1).

Stern, D. 1985. *The interpersonal world of the infant* New York: Basic Books.

Stoehr, T. 1994. *Here, now, next: Paul Goodman and the origins of Gestalt therapy*. San Francisco: Jossey-Bass.

Straus, E. 1997/1952. *Le soupir, introduction à une théorie de l'expression*. Bordeaux: Presses de l'IFGT.

Tatossian, A. 1996. Les conditions aprioriques d'une psychothérapie des schizophrènes. *L'Art du Comprendre* 5/6w.

Touraine, A. 1992. *Critique de la modernité*. Paris: Fayard.

Tournier, M. 1972. *Vendredi ou les limbes du pacifique*. Paris: Gallimard.

Viderman, S. 1970. *La construction de l'espace analytique*. Paris: TEL-Gallimard.

Wheeler, G. 1996. Self and shame: a new paradigm for psychotherapy. In *The Voice of Shame*, edited by Lee, R. W., G. San Francisco: Jossey-Bass.

Wittgenstein, L. 1922. *Tractatus Logico Philosophicus*. London: Routledge & Kegan Paul.

———. 1961. *Investigations philosophiques*. Paris: Gallimard. Original edition, 1953.

Wittgenstein, Ludwig. 1989. *Remarques sur la philosophie de la psychologie*. Mauvezin: Trans-Europ-Repress.

Yontef, G.M. 1988. Comments on 'Boundary processes and boundary states. *The Gestalt Journal* 11 (2).

———. 1993. *Awareness, dialogue and process: Essays on Gestalt therapy*. Gouldsboro, ME: The Gestalt Journal Press.

INDEX